THE
LITTLE
BOOK
OF
IRELAND

C.M. BOYLAN

The
History
Press
Ireland

To Andy, for everything.

First published 2013

The History Press Ireland
50 City Quay
Dublin 2
Ireland
www.thehistorypress.ie

© C.M. Boylan, 2013
Illustrations © Catherine Cox

British Library Cataloguing in Publication Data.
A catalogue record for this book is available from the British Library.

ISBN 978 1 84588 804 6

Typesetting and origination by The History Press

CONTENTS

Acknowledgements   4

Introduction   5

1.   Geography   7

2.   People   28

3.   Culture   47

4.   Sport and Leisure   66

5.   Food and Drink   75

6.   Education   85

7.   Law   94

8.   Religion   105

9.   Transport, Communication and Science   115

10.   Wars and Rebellions   126

      Conclusion   144

ACKNOWLEDGEMENTS

Thanks to all of the following for their help and suggestions: Andy Donald, Tom Boylan, Noeleen Boylan, Aileen Donald, Declan Burke, Seán King, Treasa de Loughry, Avril Conry, Aoife Conry, Elaine Dobbyn, Fionnán Nestor, Eimear Grealy, Honor Griffin.

Quotation from Seamus Heaney's 'Lovers in Aran' by kind permission of Faber & Faber.

INTRODUCTION

A little book about a little country should be a relatively simple and manageable affair. However, Ireland has always somehow seemed like a big country. This is probably due mainly to the size of what is called 'The Irish Diaspora': those millions who left the island to settle abroad and the succeeding generations who lay claim to Irish roots. The size of this diaspora is quite astonishing considering the fact that the population of Ireland has never been more than about 8.2 million people. In the period between 1815 and 1921 it is estimated that 8 million people left Ireland permanently so that, by 1990, the President at the time, Mary Robinson, could state that across the world there were over 70 million persons claiming at least partial Irish descent. The presence of these millions – who scattered mainly to the United States, Canada, Australia and Great Britain – has always made Ireland seem bigger than it really is. The fact that virtually every US President (or so it seems) has claimed Irish roots is testament to this 'diaspora effect' (as well as to the tenacity of Irish genealogists in claiming VIPs).

The second aggrandising factor is the border between the Republic of Ireland and Northern Ireland. The Troubles, that period of bitter conflict and violence between the late 1960s and 1998, was like listening to a shrill, atonal recording of the animosities of several centuries being played on repeat day after day. The Troubles made international headlines both for the carnage that was wreaked and, eventually, for the success of the

Peace Process. All of this certainly served to make Ireland, and her history, seem like the very opposite of little and insignificant.

We might conclude that despite being only the twentieth largest island in the world and the hundred and twentieth largest country, with a highest elevation of only 3,400ft, this little island has either a disproportionately large history, culture and society or a disproportionately large sense of its own importance.

This book contains some selected facts about Ireland. The facts are, if you like, jigsaw pieces that can be put together to make a picture of Ireland. The task of fitting the pieces together is left entirely to the reader. It should also be noted that the facts chosen may not always be familiar and the lesser known has been mixed with the better known. This is not done in an effort to avoid familiar narratives but in an effort to persuade the shyer facts to put their heads around the door and step outside.

The facts are assembled under various thematic headings and they testify to various idiosyncrasies, quirks and peculiarities of the country and its people. Indeed, the Irish are quite fond of reminding people of their exceptionality and uniqueness. The flip side of this argument is that few Irish people look outside Ireland to see if this really is exceptionality or merely an Irish version of the funfair of human history and existence. Whether Ireland and the Irish truly are unique is not for this book to pontificate upon. It is up to the reader to decide if the facts within amount to a collection of differences or a collection of samenesses.

What will be said, however, is that it is a wonderful and great country and if there are any singularities and differences unique to Ireland then these should surely be cherished and celebrated. We should come ashore on these differences like tired sailors onto sandy islands in the middle of vast oceans.

1

GEOGRAPHY

A CONVERSATION WITH A GLOBE

If a globe of the world could talk it might start immediately to tell you about the colossal continent of Africa that it carries with pride on its back: huge, varied Africa with its infinities of sand, its wide plains and its steaming tropical rains. Or it might want to tell you about the massive swathe of land called Russia that it has heaved onto its shoulders; about the miles and miles of snow and tundra to the north or the vast grain fields in the south. And if you interrupted it and asked it to focus on Europe, it would probably start to talk about the breath-stealing beauty of the snow-capped Alps; the great rivers with their verdant banks; or the peculiarity of the boot-shaped country that stretches its limb into the heaven-reflecting azure of the Mediterranean.

'But what about Ireland?' you might ask.

'That small rock on the edge?' it might reply. 'That island has a total area of 84,421 sq. km and lies between 51° and 55° north latitude and 5° and 10° west longitude', it might tell you importantly (and if it had glasses it might push them up its nose at this point).

'Those are interesting facts,' you might say, 'But can you describe it to me in your own words?'

And so the globe might relax a little bit and tell you the following: 'Ireland is grassy and rocky; lush and barren;

fantastically wild and sedately pastoral. It's not very big though, about 480km at its longest and 275km at its widest. People often say it is shaped like a saucer: higher around the edges, flatter in the middle.

'Two of the great European mountain systems meet in Ireland: the ancient Caledonian mountains that stretch themselves across the north of the country and into the west, forming the worn conical peaks of the Twelve Bens, Croagh Patrick and lonely Errigal. The younger Armorican mountains extend across the south and peak in the Magillycuddy's reeks. Carrantouhill, at 1,041m tall, is Ireland's highest heaven-grazing point. The middle of the country is a lowland that is open to the sea in the east from the Wicklow Mountains to the Carlingford peninsula (a stretch of 90km). This lowland stretches all the way over to the west coast, finding its way between mountains and hills to outlets in the Shannon Estuary, Galway Bay, Clew Bay and Donegal Bay.

'Ireland shivered under ice in what scientists call the Pleistocene era, but that melted about 12,000 years ago, leaving behind

... grassy and rocky; lush and barren

reminders of a time when glaciers lay sleeping across the land: look at the drumlins of Monaghan, the valley of Glendalough or Esker Riada. There are numerous streams and rivers flowing and winding their way across the face of the island, of which the longest is the mighty river Shannon which, at 358m, is the longest in either Ireland or Britain.

'The climate is mild, mainly owing to the relatively warm waters of the North Atlantic Drift that rush up to hug the west and south coasts. The yearly temperature range is really very small and extremes are virtually unknown, although to listen to the human inhabitants, you would not get this impression as they always appear to be labouring under personal extremities of cold or heat.

'What they often are, however, is wet, although certain parts of the country are showered more regularly. While rainfall in the east might be between 750 and 1,000mm per year, in the west it averages 1,000 to 1,400mm. While the number of wet days along the east and south east coast is 150, in some parts of the west it is about 225 days. The main feature of the weather is changeability and although this might make activities hard to plan and render the islanders' moods as unpredictable as the heavens, anyone who has seen the colour kaleidoscope in Connemara over the course of a day will agree that there is beauty in constant change.

'The vibrant green of the island is because of the plentiful grasses that grow well in the mild, moist conditions. There is a relative lack of trees, however, especially along the wind-blasted western coast. Extensive oak woodlands stretched across the midlands in a bygone age; most of these were cleared centuries ago. The flora is, admittedly, a bit limited, though there are notable exceptions. There is the bare, rocky karst landscape of the Burren in County Clare, where Arctic and Alpine flowers grow in the cracks; the great-great-grandchildren of flowers from an older and colder time. And in the extreme south-west of Kerry and Cork warm microclimates allow Mediterranean-type vegetation to grow.

'As for the creatures that roam on the island: there are twenty-seven species of mammal. Native to Ireland are the red deer, pine martin, badger, otter, hare and stoat. Introduced are the fallow deer, rabbit and other rodents. The fresh waters teem with salmon, trout, char, polan, perch, pike and eels while there are

380 species of wild birds. Around the coasts, seals breed and whales sometimes pass close by.

'It may not be as big or as dramatic as some of the other places I carry, but that small rock is a gem.'

MAPS

Ptolemy

The most detailed early description of Ireland appears in Ptolemy's *Geography*, dating from about AD 150. The original maps Ptolemy included have not survived, but over the centuries maps were drawn based on the coordinates and information he provided. Ireland is recognisably itself; which is impressive when you consider that the maps produced in Ptolemy's workshop in Alexandria, were based purely on his astronomical/mathematical calculations combined with the accounts of sailors, traders and military personnel. Even more surprising is that quite a few rivers can be identified with certainty from Ptolemy's depiction. Fifteen are shown, including the Shannon, the Boyne and the Lee. Howth and Rathlin islands are there, as is the Isle of Mann and the Hebrides (though these are just off the north-east coast). The map also notes kingdoms and royal centres and is thus a very early record of the political order; older than the earliest native Irish records.

Portolan Charts

Ireland also appeared in the medieval *mappa mundi* and portolan charts. While the *mappa mundi* were often based on theological beliefs, the portolan charts were produced by mariners from the thirteenth century, for the wholly practical purpose of navigation. They were based on direct observation and first-hand experience and, given their users, note only coastal locations while the interiors are left largely unfurnished. In one map from 1561 Ireland is shown with St Patrick's Purgatory, a legendary lake said to contain over 300 islands, as the dominant feature. Its appearance in numerous portolan charts show how little knowledge there was about Ireland.

DOWN SURVEY

The Confederate Wars of 1641–53 (which included the Cromwellian conquest of Ireland), were followed by confiscations of land from Catholics. These allowed the English Commonwealth to repay the soldiers who had fought in the wars and the creditors of the conquest. There were a number of surveys undertaken to value the land in connection with this: the Gross Survey of 1653, the Civil Survey of 1654 and the Down Survey of 1656–58. This latter was an impressive endeavour: a systematic mapping of an area this large on such a scale had never been attempted before. It set the standard for future colonial surveys. It was called the Down Survey because of the system of putting down chains to measure the land to a scale of 40 perches to 1 inch (the modern equivalent of 1:50,000). It was headed up by William Petty, physician-in-chief to the Cromwellian army. In 1685 Petty used the survey to create the first printed atlas of Irish provinces and counties, *Hiberniae Delineatio.*

Ordnance Survey

Another great feat of mapping was accomplished with the Ordnance Survey of Ireland (tracings of parish maps of the Down Survey were used to create the first Ordnance Survey maps). The Ordnance Survey Office was established in 1824 to map the land in order to value it for taxation purposes. The first survey, completed at a scale of 6 to 1, was finished in 1849, making Ireland the first country to be mapped on such a detailed scale. The Survey is still headquartered in its original base of Mountjoy House in the Phoenix Park.

DESCRIPTIONS

Early Description

One of the earliest depictions of Ireland in writing came from the first-century Roman author Strabo, who situated Ireland to the north of Britain, at the edge of the known world. He described the inhabitants as 'more Savage than the Britons' before going on to describe their cannibalism of their own dead fathers and their incest with their mothers and sisters, before honourably adding the caveat that 'I say this only with the understanding that I have no trustworthy witnesses for it'.

Gerald of Wales

A more fulsome depiction of Ireland came from Giraldus Cambrensis or Gerald of Wales. He was a member of a powerful Anglo-Norman family and was related to some of those involved in the Norman invasion of 1169. He was very well educated and paid two visits to Ireland – one around 1182 and the second in 1185 – the product of which was two books: *Topographia Hiberniae* and *Expugnatio Hibernica* (or *The Topography of Ireland* and *The Conquest of Ireland*). His accounts, given his background, were hardly likely to be objective. It has been argued that Gerald's descriptions were an archetype of colonialist description: depicting the natives as backward beyond belief and thereby justifying invasion on the grounds of civilisation.

Though he admitted that the Irish were 'tall and handsome ... with agreeable and ruddy countenances' he was adamant that 'their want of civilisation, shown both in their dress and mental culture makes them a barbarous people'. He describes 'a people that has not yet departed from the primitive habits of pastoral life'. The Irish, by all accounts, were too lazy to plant fruit trees, to mine for metals, to manufacture flax or wool, or to engage in any kind of trade or mechanical art. They didn't appear interested in either proper agricultural labour or the 'wealth of towns' or civil institutions, but preferred to cling on to their old habits rather than embrace anything new. Thus, the usual progression of mankind from forest to field to town to civilisation eluded them.

Is it any wonder they exhibited such habits of barbarism when 'habits are formed by mutual intercourse; and as these people inhabit a country so remote from the rest of the world and lying at its furthest extremity, forming as it were, another world, and are thus excluded from civilised nations'. As a result, he noted, 'they learn nothing and practise nothing, but the barbarism in which they are born and bred and which sticks to them like a second nature'. He concluded, 'Whatever natural gifts they possess are excellent, in whatever requires industry they are worthless'. Certainly, the same kinds of arguments were still being endlessly spouted in the nineteenth century: the colonised country was viewed as somewhere with so much untapped potential if only the feckless masses would hoist themselves out of the ruts they had been idling in for centuries!

Giraldus also provided what must be one of the most literal depictions of a hermaphrodite in existence: 'On the right side of her face she had a long and thick beard, which covered both sides of her lips to the middle of her chin, like a man; on the left, her lips and chin were smooth and hairless, like a woman'. Perhaps unsurprisingly, this does not appear to have been a first-hand account.

Fynes Moryson

Fynes Moryson was stationed in Ireland for three years from 1600 as personal secretary to Lord Mountjoy, the Lord Deputy of Ireland, during the Nine Years War (1594–1603). Distinguishing between the 'mere Irish' and the 'English-Irish', he concentrated his description on the former. Overall, his description was not flattering.

The Irish were 'by nature extremely given to idleness' which 'makes them also slovenly and sluttish in their houses and apparel, so as upon every hill they lie *lousing* themselves'. The Irish are fast runners, courageous fighters, and excellent harpists, having a great love of music. They are given to hyperbole: he noted that men had stood in front of the Lord Deputy petitioning for justice for those who had murdered them.

Physically Irish men and women were 'large for bigness and stature' but 'generally the very men are observed to have little and ladylike hands and feet' while the greatest part of the women 'have very great *dugs*, some so big as they give their children such over their shoulders'. Incidentally, the reason the Irish were so strapping, according to Moryson, was because they were brought up in freedom with loose clothing.

With regard to their clothes, 'The men wear long and large shirts, coloured with saffron, a preservation against lice, they being seldom or never washed'. The women wear yards of linen on their heads, 'as the women do in Turkey'; and wear so many bracelets and necklaces, 'as rather load than adorn'.

The Irish were 'fruitful in generation' and he noted some cases of multiple births. Given their fertility it was probably a good thing that Irish women apparently found childbirth such a breezy undertaking. Within two hours of giving birth they were often found eating and drinking with ladies who have come to visit them, while one soldier's wife marched 6 miles from one camping place to the next the same day she gave birth. Indeed, midwives and neighbours came to help a woman in labour 'commonly more for fashion than any great need of them'. Many Irish women might wonder where this physical capacity has gone.

As for male-female relations we get this: 'The men, as well mere Irish as the old inhabitants of the English-Irish, hold it a shame to go abroad or walk with their wives, and much more to ride before them on horseback'. He adds, 'They hold it a disgrace to ride upon a mare'.

The Irish seldom eat wild fowl or fish being too lazy to catch them. At feasts, both the mere Irish and English-Irish 'have the German fashion of putting frolics about the table, as pinching and kissing over the shoulders, and many strange ways'.

As for pastimes, it seems the Irish loved gambling at cards and dice. Perhaps too much since they did not just play for all the money and clothes they had, he notes, 'but even for the members of their body at a rate of money, suffering themselves to be tied by those members and to be led about till they can free them by paying the rate of money'. Despite gambling away arms and legs, they also delighted in dancing.

They were 'much annoyed with innumerable wolves' eating their cattle but were, of course, too idle to make any effort to destroy them.

Ludolf von Münchhausen

In case one might be tempted to blame an Anglo bias for the opinions above, there is this unflattering impression of the Irish from the German Ludolf von Münchhausen in 1591:

> The people are dirty, uncouth and lazy. They have brains enough for roguery, but are ignorant of arts and the more subtle craftsmanship. They delight in idleness, they are no good for work; rather than cultivate their fields they stay at home and rest around their fires, barely dressed. I myself have seen how seven people have dragged at one piece of timber without hardly moving it.

He concluded, unimpressed, 'I would have been well able to move it on my own'.

Von Müchhausen echoed a lot of Moryson's observations. Everything was filthy amongst the Irish: their food, their clothes, their jugs. Women who had just given birth had then to walk for miles. They were again noted to wear linen cloths around their heads, which would be pretty if only they were clean and dressed differently.

Johann Friedrich Hering

Johann Friedrich Hering wrote his impressions in 1806–1807. Arriving in Dublin he remarked that it was more beautiful than London, though lacking the latter's splendour and wealth. He then headed west to Connacht.

He noted that opulence existed right alongside the deepest poverty in Ireland. The countryside was neglected, poorly cultivated and dotted with 'wretched mud-cabins'. He provided a description of a mud-cabin:

> only from six to eight feet high and 12 feet square, built of mud and straw, or of stone without any kind of cement, and covered with sods ... Light enters those cabins through gaps left unclosed and in bad weather stopped up with straw, or through a small pane that has been fixed in.

So much for the exterior. The interior had, 'in one corner a bed of straw for humans, in another a sow with young, an ass, goats and such like, and in the third a table, chair and spinning-wheel'. The family would sit in the middle of the floor around the turf-fire, 'where the husband and wife smoke their little pipe'. The fourth corner contained the exit and entrance. 'I admit there are also exceptions but rarely', he noted.

He was alarmed at the backwardness, remarking on the evident poverty of the peasantry and their unsophisticated farming tools as a result of which they had to work the land laboriously. There was no plough and horse, for instance; everything was done with a spade. Instead of vehicles to transport things, 'On pitiable, rough horses or asses led by straw-ropes hung a pair of baskets in which dung, turf and suchlike were being transported'. He noted that the 'people of rank and the well-to-do' stay mostly in Dublin or London, only going to the countryside to collect their rents which they spend abroad, 'which may contribute greatly to the poverty'.

DIVISIONS

Historically Ireland was divided into some 65,000 administrative units: 4 provinces, 32 counties, around 275 baronies, 2,400 civil parishes and around 62,000 townlands.

Provinces

Ireland is divided into four provinces: Connacht, Leinster, Ulster and Munster. The suffix '*ster*' is Norman French for 'land'. Thus, Leinster is the land of the Laighin, one of the earliest Celtic tribes to arrive; Munster is the land of Mumhain, a derivation of the pre-Celtic goddess Muma; Ulster is the land of the Ulaidh. Connacht is derived from Connachta, the dominant tribe in the early centuries of the first millennium.

There was once a fifth province: Midh meaning middle and it took in present-day Meath, Westmeath and part of Offaly.

Counties

The division of Ireland into counties took place piecemeal from the twelfth to the seventeenth centuries as the country came under English control. Dublin was a shire by 1190s while Wicklow was the last county to be created in 1606.

The county system followed the British system of shire government and counties were used as administrative divisions. Ironically, the fierce loyalty people feel towards this essentially English administrative division owes more to the Gaelic revivalism of the GAA, which made the county their organisational unit, than anything else.

Townlands

Muckanaghederdauhaulia is the longest place name in Ireland at twenty-two letters. A townland in Connemara, in Irish it is

'Muiceanach idir Dhá Sháile'; literally 'pig-shaped hill between two seas'. Two other townland names of the same length have also been registered: Glassillaunvealnacurra, County Galway and Illaungraffanavrankagh, County Clare.

Towns

We all know that the name Dublin is derived from the Irish '*Dubhlinn*', which translates as 'black pool' but there are other towns in Ireland too, a surprising amount of which also have names (all, in fact).

Cork is derived from the Irish '*Corcach*' meaning 'marsh'. Cork grew up around the monastery founded by St Finbar, which was built on the edge of a marsh. Part of Cork City is still called 'The Marsh'.

The area of Dublin known as Irishtown, between Ringsend and Sandymount, got its name after the English authorities in fifteenth-century Dublin became alarmed by the influx of Gaelic Irish migrants to the city. Concerned that the English language and English culture would become a minority presence within the city, they insisted that the Gaelic Irish be removed. This took place about 1454. They were allowed to trade within the city during daylight hours and afterwards retreated to their new base in Irishtown, just outside the city walls.

The town of Horseleap on the Offaly and Westmeath border, derives its name from an athletic horse. The local lord, Hugh de Lacy, fleeing from the MacGeoghans, arrived at his castle to find the drawbridge up. He leapt across the moat on his horse to safety.

Donnybrook in Dublin is a corruption of '*Domhnac na mBroc*' or 'Sunday of the badgers'. This comes from a horrible entertainment that saw a badger placed in a barrel lying on its side. Dogs were sent into the barrel, one by one, mostly emerging bloodied and beaten, until eventually the poor creature was worn down.

Evidently all towns are new towns at some point in their existence (generally towards the beginning of it); however, some new towns have more interesting stories than others. New Tipperary was built around 1890 by the evicted tenants of a local estate. In 1888–89, the tenants of landlord Arthur Barry Smith withheld their rents in solidarity with tenants on

his Cork estate. After their eviction, and under the direction of Fr David Humphreys and William O'Brien, they began to build a new town on land outside his control. With the help of money raised in America and Australia and labour from the surrounding villages, New Tipperary was built as a testament to tenant solidarity at the highpoint of the Plan of Campaign. Smith Barry's tenants left their shops and houses in the centre of town and moved to New Tipperary on the site of present-day Dillon Street and Emmet Street. William O'Brien Arcade – a row of shops for these business people – was opened in April 1890. Eventually a compromise was reached and the residents agreed to return to 'Old Tipperary'.

ISLANDS

Mythical Islands

Tír na nÓg
Many cultures have tales about islands: lost islands, islands buried beneath the waves, magical islands, or mirage islands. Ireland has Tír na nÓg, 'Land of the Young'. Tír na nÓg is a paradise island

located off the west coast where time doesn't play its cruel game. According to the legend, the poet-warrior Óisín met the beautiful Niamh Chinn Óir (Niamh of the Golden Hair) on a white horse, who took him across the sea to Tír na nÓg where he lived in a timeless land where death, sickness, want and unhappiness were unknown, until eventually he felt the keen loss of his loved ones and asked to return. Niamh gave him the white horse but told him that if he set foot on Irish soil he would not be allowed to come back. Óisín travelled home and was aggrieved to see that so much time had passed without his noticing, that all his people had passed on and that the land had changed. He came across some men trying to move a boulder. Being famed for his strength, he leant from the horse to move the stone but slipped and fell to the ground. He aged in an instant. According the legend, he was taken to see a holy man before he died and recounted his fantastical story. The holy man was St Patrick.

Hy Brasil

> On the ocean that hollows the rocks where ye dwell
> A shadowy land has appeared as they tell;
> Men thought it a region of sunshine and rest,
> And they called it Hy-Brasil, the Isle of the Blest.

Gerald Griffin, 'Hy-Brasil, the Isle of the Blest'

Another legendary island, but one that appeared on real maps, was Hy Brasil. Hy Brasil was located on maps from the fourteenth century, situated off the west coast. The name seems to have been derived from Middle Irish. '*Hy*' was derived from 'í' meaning 'island'. Brasil comes from the root '*bres*' meaning 'mighty, great, beautiful'. The island is also associated with the Celtic god Breasal and the high king of the Celtic world, Bresal, who established his court on the island of Bresal.

The mythical island appears in many legends and stories as a paradise island and even as a submerged land of virtue and Christian faith concealed beneath the waves. It first appeared on a real map in 1325 and, astonishingly, was not removed from British

Admiralty charts until 1870. One reason is that the island moved around (it appeared among the Canaries, Azores and Madeira and even off Canada), although for the most part it remained off the Irish coast. The other reason is that it was continually sighted by sailors, despite not existing. It was kept alive in the legends because it was a land of bliss and in the stories of sailors because it offered hope of a stop-off point in the age of sea-faring discovery or a land to be discovered and colonised in its own right.

Real Islands
There are over 300 islands of varying sizes off Ireland's coastline.

Lambay
Lambay lies off the coast of north County Dublin; the largest island off the east coast and the most easterly point in Ireland. It has had a very colourful history. St Columba was supposed to have established a monastery on the island around 530. During the Williamite wars, the island was used as an internment camp for Irish soldiers. Over 1,000 were imprisoned there after the Battle of Aughrim (1691) where some died of their wounds or starvation. The island is currently a private island, owned by the Baring family trust (Cecil Baring, later Lord Revelstoke, bought the island in 1904) and can only be accessed by prior permission. It is probably just as well that visitor numbers are kept down in this way as the island is an extraordinary wildlife reserve. It is the largest seabird colony in Ireland, home to over 50,000 common guillemots, 5,000 kittiwakes, 3,500 razorbills, 2,500 pairs of herring gulls, as well as smaller numbers of puffins, Manx shearwaters, fulmars, and other species. The island is not, contrary to some wishful reports, also home to kangaroos and wallabies.

Tory Island
An English visitor to Tory island, off the north-west coast of Donegal, in 1834 noted that the islanders elected a 'chief judge' who issued his mandate from a 'throne of turf' to their ready obedience. To this day Tory elects a king (Rí Thoraí), who, though he does not have any formal powers, acts as a spokesperson for the island community.

Valentia
In 1993 a geology undergraduate stumbled upon some fossilised tetrapod trackways on Valentia Island, County Kerry. About 385 million years ago, when this part of Ireland was an equatorial swamp, a primitive vertebrate made the footprints, which turned out to be amongst the oldest signs of vertebrate life ever discovered.

The famous Valentia Slate, mined from the quarry that opened in 1816, has been used in the construction of many buildings included the British Houses of Parliament.

Inishboffin
The island of Inishboffin off the County Galway coast was used by Cromwell's parliamentarian forces as a prison for Catholic priests rounded up across Ireland. The star-shaped barracks known as 'Cromwell's Barracks' was also used to protect the coast against pirates and Dutch raiders, since Cromwell's Protectorate were at war with Holland.

Rathlin
The first recorded Viking raid took place on Rathlin Island off the Antrim coast in AD 795.

The Blaskets
Great Blasket island is remarkable in producing three of the best known and respected writers in the Irish language, who depicted the harsh realities of island life in their works: Peig Sayers (*Peig*), Tomás Ó Criomhthain (*An tOileánach* or *The Islandman*) and Muiris Ó Suilleabháin (*Fiche Blian ag Fás* or *Twenty Years A-Growing*). Islands were always harsh economic climates. The Blasket islands were evacuated on 17 November 1953 and all the inhabitants moved to the mainland in scenes repeated amongst island communities up and down the coast.

FACTS ABOUT THE COAST

Ireland's oldest operational lighthouse was built at Hook Head, County Wexford, in the twelfth century. This was apparently on the site where the monks of St Dubhan tended a fire beacon in the fifth century.

Ireland's last manned lighthouse was Baily Lighthouse in Howth, which was fully automated in 1997.

The Ordnance Survey puts the Irish coastline at 3,171km long.

Over half of Ireland's population live within 10km of the coast.

More than 460 species of fish and 24 types of whale and dolphin have been recorded around Ireland.

FACTS ABOUT THE LAND

Lough Neagh is the largest lake in both Ireland or Britain. Lough Corrib, County Galway, is the second largest.

The geographical centre of Ireland is found in County Roscommon, 3km south of Athlone.

There are 849 towns and cities in Ireland as of the 2011 census, up from 747 in 2006.

The population density of Ireland is 67 persons per km².

In 2010, 10.7 per cent of the land was covered by forestry, the second lowest percentage of forest cover in the European Union.

BOGS

Ireland's bogs started their slow process of creation 9,000 years ago.

Ireland has more bog per capita than any other European country except Finland.

In 1986 a perfectly preserved 900-year-old cheese was pulled from a Tipperary bog. Other things found preserved in Irish bogs: bodies, weapons, parcels of butter or lard and a Book of Psalms.

At the Céide Fields in Mayo a peat-cutter in the 1930s stumbled upon an entire way of life: a 5,500 year old complex of Neolithic houses, tombs and fields surrounded by stone walls suggesting a sophisticated farming system.

POPULATION

A child will make two dishes at an entertainment for friends; and when the family dines alone, the fore or hind quarter will make a reasonable dish.

Jonathan Swift's satirical suggestion in *A Modest Proposal* (1729) that Irish children be raised for food may not have been serious, but it reflected a concern with Irish overpopulation and poverty, which were deemed to be closely related.

The Irish population in 1841, just before the Famine, was 8.1 million. In 1851 it was 6.5 million and by 1891 it had dropped to 4.7 million. Emigration was increasing before the Famine, but it greatly accelerated during and after.

This trend continued into the twentieth century and it seemed that the population was in terminal decline. Half a million people emigrated from the Republic of Ireland in the 1950s. If a young person had no land, no dowry or no prospects of a job, chances were they left on the boat. The Revd E. Noonan claimed in *The Vanishing Irish* (1954): 'It is an indisputable fact ... that the Irish are a vanishing race. If the present rate continues, they will be counted among the extinct people in less than a hundred years'.

Seán Ó Faoláin, writing in the same volume, similarly noted the torrential outflow of emigration. He also pointed to some of the reasons for the simultaneously low marriage rates in the country, which seemed be exacerbating the decline. There were ancient old men who simply refused to die and pass on the land

and livelihoods to their sons, who could therefore not begin their lives. There was also a problem with the available women, apparently. Ó Faoláin quoted one clearly exasperated Romeo:

> The average, modern Irish girl is a painted, powdered, padded, puffed parrot, except for her nails which are hawk's claws. Their adoration of film actors has reached a state of imbecility! It is often said that slow horses and fast women would ruin any man, but we don't need the horses, the women do it alone. How could any man in his sane senses, for whom marriage means a family and responsibility, contemplate a life spent with one of these lassies?

Despite these assertions the decline was in fact halted. The key moment was probably the publication of T.K. Whitaker's *Programme of Economic Expansion* in 1958 which suggested that Ireland should end her economic isolationism; that the economy should become more open, export-driven and industrialised; and that foreign investment should be encouraged. The 1960s were also a global boom time, and with these developments the tide of emigration was stemmed.

The current population of the Republic of Ireland is 4.5 million and of Northern Ireland is 1.8 million, giving a total of 6.3 million for the island.

2

PEOPLE

THE ECCENTRIC

Ireland, like anywhere inhabited by human beings, has produced its share of eccentrics.

Perhaps the greatest of these was Aldolphus Cooke (1792–1876). Cooke was born in Cookesborough, near Mullingar, the illegitimate son of Robert Cooke and a servant who was subsequently banished. Not allowed to visit his father's house, Adolphus was brought up by a nurse in a small cottage. After his father's death, he inherited the estate and there reigned in glorious eccentricity.

A former army man, he drilled his servants like they were soldiers. Repelled by children, he once gave a beggar £5 as a reward for being childless. He had a much greater regard for animals, in part due to his belief in reincarnation. He believed he would reappear as a fox or a bird and as such had a cousin disinherited for killing a fox while hunting. When a bullock was drowning, he forced the other bullocks to look on as a warning to them. Confronted once by a bull, he set to fighting it with a red coat and sword. When a maid servant intervened to rescue him, he dismissed her, noting that only the strong should survive.

The crows at Cookesborough were treated particularly well and there was a turkey-cock he believed contained the soul of his father or grandfather and which was therefore accorded special care.

He also had a favourite red setter called Gusty. Prone to roaming, Gusty was sanctioned on numerous occasions and then publicly warned that one more transgression would result in his being hanged like a common criminal. When Gusty disobeyed, he was found, hauled home and a trial was ordered. The jury heard how Gusty had resisted arrest and he was found guilty. The servants, however, were reluctant to perform the execution. Eventually a man called 'The Bug Mee' agreed. Taking the dog around the corner, he returned some time later with Gusty alive, saying that the turkey-cock had intervened in the hanging. Cooke was satisfied with this and gave the man the sole job of looking after Gusty and the turkey-cock.

Cooke had a 40 sq. ft marble vault built on the estate, complete with marble table, chairs and books. A huge fireplace within was ordered to be kept perpetually lit. After his death (the rector refused to bury him in his vault, instead burying him with his nurse and father) the cousin who had been disinherited for killing a fox contested the will, claiming that Cooke was of unsound mind. The court concluded he was not insane.

THE COLLECTOR

Charles Haliday (1789?–1866), merchant, banker, antiquarian and public health reformer, amassed a vast collection of about 38,000 pamphlets. He was so well known as a collector that the Dublin waste-paper sellers would accost him outside his office with books and pamphlets and he sent an agent to auctions for him as his presence would automatically lead prices to increase. Not only did he collect the pamphlets, he organised 22,000 of them into 2,209 bound volumes arranged chronologically and thematically within the chronology. They covered a 300-year span and subjects ranging from railways to rebellions to religion. Haliday himself was a prolific pamphleteer and letter writer, producing works on the Union, temperance and the living conditions of the poor. His wife donated his collection to the Royal Irish Academy after his death.

THE EXPLORERS

St Brendan

Perhaps the best-known explorer of them all is St Brendan 'The Navigator'. He was born in County Kerry around 483 and was known for his seafaring voyages around Britain and Ireland, venturing to Iona in Scotland and St Malo in Brittany. Shrouded in legend is his epic seven-year voyage across the ocean. According to the *Navigatio Sancti Brendani*, written about 1050, Brendan and his companions set out in his boat and reached Iceland, Greenland and even America. Mind you, they also apparently celebrated Easter on the back of a whale, fought off a giant sea horse and met Judas Iscariot clinging to a rock. Nonetheless, there may be some truth to the legend. In 1977, Tim Severin built a replica boat and sailed from Galway to Newfoundland, proving at least that it was physically possible. Brendan founded a monastery in Clonfert, Galway, in 558 where he was buried after he died in 578.

Daniel Houghton

Daniel Houghton (1740–91) was born in Ireland and entered the army where he served in Gibraltar and Morocco. Making his way to India to become an engineer, the commander of the fleet in which he was travelling captured Goree, an island off present-day Senegal, from the French. Houghton stayed on with the British garrison in various administrative posts. He travelled up the Gambia River, hoping to establish a trading post. After returning to England and finding himself in financial difficulties, he offered his services to the Association for Promoting the Discovery of the Interior Parts of Africa, also known as the Africa Association, in 1790. Houghton proposed an expedition to Timbuktu, Mali.

He arrived in Gambia with some trade goods, and set off with an interpreter, some porters and baggage animals. The journey was beset by challenges and misfortunes: he had to avoid murderous local traders who feared he would undermine their business; some of his trade goods were destroyed in a fire; his interpreter bolted with some of the animals; and he injured his face and arm when a gun exploded. He nonetheless made it to Medina and left there in May 1791, later that month reaching Bondou territory, going beyond the previous limit of European exploration. There, more of his trade goods were stolen by the son of a local king and he suffered a delirious fever but despite this reached Ferbanna, capital of the Bambouk territory, where he was received with kindness by the local king. He left Ferbanna for Timbuktu in July 1791 and was never heard from again.

His last dispatches later reached London stating that he had travelled over 1,000 miles up the Senegambia and providing much topographical information. Later, the Scottish explorer Mungo Park uncovered his steps, discovering that he had made it as far as Tarra where he was again robbed and fell ill. It is not clear whether he died of illness or starvation or was murdered but Park was shown where his body was discarded.

Edward Bransfield

The first man to sight Antarctica was an Irishman. Edward Bransfield (*c.* 1785–1852) was born in Midleton, County Cork. He was pressed into the Royal Navy at eighteen and had a very successful career. In 1817 he was appointed master of a large forty-four-gun frigate, the *Andromache*, under Captain Shirreff, which sailed to South America. There he was ordered to survey the South Shetland Islands which had been discovered the previous year by William Smith. On 22 January 1820 Bransfield and his men came into the bay of a long island which they claimed for Britain and Bransfield named New South Britain (he named the bay George's Bay, now King George's Bay). Bransfield surveyed each of the twelve South Shetland Islands.

On 30 January 1820, they sighted a high mountain range running in a north-westerly direction. This was the first reported sighting of the Antarctic Peninsula. Bransfield named it Trinity Land. He gives his name to Bransfield Strait, Bransfield Island and Bransfield Rocks off the coast of the Antarctic Peninsula and Mount Bransfield on Trinity. He left the navy the following year, re-joined the merchant service and eventually retired to Brighton, Sussex.

Tom Crean

Kerryman Tom Crean (1877–1938) spent more time in the Antarctic than either R.F. Scott or Ernest Shackleton (another Irishman). He was on Scott's British National Antarctic Expedition of 1901–04 after which he was awarded the Polar medal. He took part in the ill-fated British Antarctic Expedition of 1910–13. He was one of the last to see Scott and his men alive and was one of the search party who discovered their bodies in November 1912. He was awarded the Albert Medal for travelling eighteen hours in a blizzard to get help for his team leader who had taken ill.

Returning to England in 1913, he immediately signed up for another expedition: Shackleton's 1914–1916 expedition where he was central in the rescue of the crew of the *Endurance*, which was beset by ice. A very modest man, Crean left the navy in 1920 and opened a small public house very near where he was born in Annascaul, County Kerry, with his wife Ellen, which he called the South Pole Inn. The Crean Glacier on South Georgia and Mount Crean in Antarctica are named in his honour.

THE EMIGRANTS

The first person to be processed through Ellis Island immigration station in New York was Annie Moore on 1 January 1892, which was also Annie's fifteenth birthday. Annie and her two younger brothers had set sail from Cobh (then called Queenstown), spending twelve days at sea and arriving on 31 December 1891. Annie was one of 148 steerage passengers on the steamship *Nevada*. They were reunited with their parents who were already living in New York. 'A ROSY-CHEEKED IRISH GIRL THE FIRST REGISTERED' read the *New York Times* article of 2 January. She was presented with at $10 gold coin ('She says she will never part with it, but will always keep it as a pleasant memento of the occasion'). Annie is commemorated in two statues: one at Cobh and one at Ellis Island.

According to the same report, the first ticket sold by the railroad agents at the new Ellis Island building was bought by Ellen King, from Waterford, on her way to a small town in Minnesota.

THE LOVERS

Sarah Ponsonby was born in Dublin in 1755. Her father was a landowner and her mother the daughter of a clerk of the Irish Privy Council. After she was orphaned, she was sent to live with her father's cousin, Lady Betty Fownes, and her husband, Sir William, at Woodstock, County Kilkenny. She attended Miss Parke's boarding school in Kilkenny city. At the age of thirteen she met the person who was to become her life partner. Eleanor Butler, of old Catholic gentry stock, was sixteen years Sarah's senior. In 1778 she declared her intention 'to live and die with Miss Butler' and in March of that year, they made their first failed attempt to elope. She apparently leapt from her window dressed in men's clothes, with a pistol and a small dog, Frisk. Their attempt foiled, Eleanor was packed off to a relative in County Carlow but escaped in May and went to find Sarah in Woodstock. Their families eventually capitulated to their wishes and they travelled to Wales and from there began a grand tour.

In 1780 they set up in a small cottage in Wales where they remained, becoming known as the refined and cultured 'Ladies of Llangollen'. Their lesbianism was not widely acknowledged. Instead, they were referred to as 'romantic friends' (though Samuel Johnson's friend Hester Thrale decried them as 'damned Sapphists'). An article in the *General Evening Post* in 1790, entitled 'Extraordinary female affection', alluded indirectly to the nature of their relationship.

They lived reclusively but their eccentricities, short cropped hair and masculine style of dress gained them notoriety and visiting them became fashionable. They played host to various distinguished visitors including William Wordsworth, Charles Darwin, Walter Scott, Edmund Burke, Arthur Wellesley (later Duke of Wellington) and Lady Caroline Lamb. Having little income other than their respective allowances and a royal pension that Eleanor received, they were often in financial difficulty.

Eleanor died in 1829 and Sarah in 1831. They were buried together, along with their faithful maid, Mary Carryll.

THE POLITICIANS

Lord Morpeth

Not all British politicians who administered Ireland were despised. Lord Morpeth (1802–64), for one, was evidently quite popular. He was Chief Secretary for Ireland from 1835 until he lost his parliamentary seat in Yorkshire in 1841. A testimonial to him was signed by over 165,000 people. The 652 sheets of paper were joined together, rolled onto a mahogany spool and presented to him. The 'Morpeth Roll' measured 420m (or, three times the length of Croke Park and not far off the height of the Empire State Building) and has some well-known signatures including Daniel O'Connell, Thomas Davis and Charles Gavan Duffy. Arguably, one of the more impressive 'Sorry you are leaving' cards ever produced.

Arthur MacMurrough Kavanagh

Arthur MacMurrough Kavanagh (1831–89) was born at Borris House, County Carlow. His father was a landowner and MP. Arthur was born with stumps in place of his arms and legs. Despite his disability, he became an accomplished horseman, learned to write with his mouth and to paint, fish, shoot and sail with competence. He also excelled at his studies as a boy. After a tryst with a local girl was interrupted by his mother, he was sent away on a long trip with his older brother and a Revd Wood. They travelled to Moscow, then down the Volga to Persia (Iran). Having developed a fever, Prince Mirza of Mosul invited him to rest for a few weeks in his harem, an offer he readily accepted, to the reverend's horror. They eventually travelled to India where Arthur fulfilled an ambition to hunt tigers, killing several, often from an elephant's back. Thomas, his brother, went on to Australia. Arthur supported himself for a year, working as a despatch messenger for the East India Company before eventually returning to Ireland on hearing of his brother's death.

He was dismayed at the effect of the Famine on the family estate. On his other brother's death, he took over the running of the estate. He proved himself very active, redesigning the village of Borris and Ballyragget; designing a slate-roofed cottage; and becoming a local magistrate, chairman of the New Ross board of guardians, JP for Carlow, Kilkenny and Wexford and high sheriff of Kilkenny and Carlow. He also married and had six children. He eventually stood as a Conservative MP in the Wexford by-election of 1866. His impairment was never an issue during the campaign and he was cheered when he was wheeled into the House of Commons to sign the register of new members. He took the seat for Carlow in 1868, running unopposed. As an MP he lobbied for various Irish causes such as lighthouses and railways and was particularly interested in the Land Question. In 1880, though he assumed his tenants would vote for him under the new secret ballot system, he found himself resoundingly defeated. He felt this as a deep betrayal. He continued his interest in public affairs, especially the land issue, and was appointed to the privy council in 1886.

Alfie Byrne

Alfred 'Alfie' Byrne (1882–1956) was elected as a Westminster MP (1915), a Dáil Éireann TD (1922–28, 1932–56), and a Senator (1928–31). He was also Mayor of Dublin ten times, from 1930 to 1939 and again in 1954. Known as 'The shaking hand of Dublin' he was as committed to his constituents (especially the poor) as he was to his own political career. He even put himself forward as a possible Presidential candidate; not bad for the son of a docker who left school at thirteen.

THE VISITORS

Although the Irish are well known for travelling abroad (very often, it must be said, to eke out a living), the country has attracted numerous interesting visitors over the centuries. Some even made their homes in Ireland.

Friedrich Engels

Friedrich Engels (1820–95) visited Ireland on a number of occasions. On his first trip in 1856 he travelled with his partner Mary Burn (a Manchester-Irish woman) from Dublin to Galway, then on to Limerick and Killarney and back to Dublin. In a letter to Karl Marx he described the appalling condition of the bulk of the population, who he felt had been systematically oppressed until 'they have come to be a completely wretched nation and now, as everyone knows, they have the job of providing England, America, Australia, etc., with whores, day labourers, maquereaux, pickpockets, swindlers, beggars and other wretches'. Quite an export trade.

He described the bleak landscape in and around Galway and the devastation that famine, emigration and clearances had reaped, noting 'I never understood before that famine could be such a tangible reality'.

His description of the landowning class at the time was what one might safely call scathing:

> These fellows are too funny for words: of mixed blood, for the most part tall, strong, handsome types, all with enormous moustaches under a vast Roman nose, they give themselves the bogus martial airs of a *colonel en retraite*, travel the country in search of every imaginable diversion and, on inquiry, prove to be as poor as church mice, up to their eyes in debt, and living in constant fear of the Encumbered Estates Court.

On a visit in 1869, Engels offered the following opinion in another letter to Marx:

> The worst about the Irish is that they become corruptible as soon as they stop being peasants and turn bourgeois. True, this is the case with most peasant nations. But in Ireland it is particularly bad.

Bruce Ismay

One of the most notorious businessmen of the early twentieth century was Bruce Ismay (1862–1937) chairman and Chief Executive of White Star Lines, whose vision had built the *Titantic* and whose actions on its sinking condemned him to infamy for the rest of his life. On the night of 14 April 1912, as the ship sank, Ismay helped women and children on to Collapsible Lifeboat C and, with nobody else in the vicinity, climbed into the boat himself along with another first class passenger, William Carter. Women and children remained on the ship and over 1,500 died. It was Ismay who had ordered the number of lifeboats to be reduced from forty-six to sixteen to make room for various luxury features that formed part of his pioneering vision of ocean travel. Ismay subsequently testified before two inquiries, in New York and London, running gauntlets of jeering crowds in New York. He was hounded and savaged by the press in America and Britain for his cowardice and was shunned from London society. He eventually retreated to Costello Lodge, Casla, in Connemara, where he lived for twenty-five years with his wife. The Ismay's were popular in the area, being good local employers and charitable. They may not, however, have known of the pun the Irish-speaking locals devised, referring to him as '*Brú síos mé*' ('lower me down', in Irish).

J.R.R. Tolkien

J.R.R. Tolkien (1892–1973)visited Ireland on many occasions and acted as external examiner for a number of Irish universities, including University College Dublin and University College Galway (now National University of Ireland, Galway), receiving an honorary degree from the National University of Ireland in 1954.

There are some who claim that the Burren in County Clare provided some inspiration for Middle Earth. Indeed there is a Burren Tolkien Society that organises a Tolkien Festival. Tolkien did visit the Burren as a guest of Professor Murphy, then head of the English Department at University College Galway, who looked after Tolkien when he visited as external examiner. Connections have been drawn between the landscape of Mordor and the Misty Mountains and that of the Burren, as well as a cave called Poll na gColm (close in sound to Gollum) and the character Gollum, not to mention the similarities with Irish folklore that have been noted. Tolkien was extern at Galway in 1949, 1950, 1954, 1958 and 1959. *The Lord of the Rings* was written between 1937 and 1949 and published in 1954.

Oswald Mosley

Oswald Mosley (1896–1990), Britain's Hitler-apparent, was interred during the Second World War for fear he would turn traitor. No doubt his society connections helped secure his early release in 1943. His first marriage had been to the daughter of Lord Curzon, former Viceroy of India and his second was to Diana, one of the Mitford sisters who were related to Churchill.

Mosley, hated in Britain, received a letter from J.D. O'Connell, the county solicitor for Kerry, in 1943 inviting him to Ireland.

In a previous incarnation as a young Conservative MP, Mosley had spoken out against the Black and Tans whose actions, he argued, were undermining the moral authority of the Empire. He favoured an arrangement whereby Ireland might be made independent, with Britain retaining a right to invade if there was any threat to her interests.

In 1946 Mosley informed the Dublin authorities that he wished to settle in Ireland. Taoiseach Éamon de Valera was consulted and Mosley's solicitor was called to the Department of Justice where it was suggested that 'The time was perhaps not opportune for him to take up permanent residence and that he might delay his decision for some time until international tempers were quieter'. Five years later, in 1951, the Oswalds took up residence in Clonfert Palace, County Galway, former home of the Trenches and residence of Church of Ireland bishops. In a statement he noted: 'Long ago I fought in parliament for the freedom of Ireland, and for the right of the Irish people to manage their own affairs. Therefore the last thing I should now try to do would be to interfere in them'. He seems to have kept to that reassuring promise, though he and his wife did continue to espouse their racist views and fraternise with aspiring European neo-fascists. In 1954, the Palace was burnt down in a fire and the Mosleys moved to Fermoy, County Cork. They kept a low profile in Ireland and seem to have been welcomed and treated well by the locals in Clonfert and Fermoy. This may have been because some Irish people were reluctant to acknowledge the extent of Nazi persecution, dismissing it as British propaganda.

The issue of immigration drew him back into British politics; specifically, the race riots in Notting Hill in 1958. This was an area where the new wave of West Indian immigrants settled alongside other white immigrants, including a large number of Irish. Mosley's Union Movement defended the mobs of racist Teddy boys. Mosley announced his intention to run in the general election of 1959 for North Kensington. In the meantime, he was up in court with his two brothers for assaulting and shooting a black medical student. At this point, TD Noel Browne, labelled him an 'undesirable' in the Dáil and expressed a fear that his residence would be used as a 'funk hole' to enable him to engage in racist activities elsewhere.

During the campaign leaflets were distributed reminding Irish voters in London that he had 'fought for them in the British parliament and lived among them in Ireland'. The election literature noted that through questioning and debate, Sir Mosley had begun the work of getting the Black and Tans out of Ireland. Now, 'The same power of question and debate can get the Blacks out of North Kensington'. Mosley received only 8 per cent of the vote.

The family spent increasing amounts of time in their Paris home and sold the house in Fermoy in 1963. Mosley returned to Ireland in 1977 for a debate with Taoiseach Jack Lynch at the King's Inn in Dublin and appeared on the *Late Late Show* with Gay Byrne. Unfortunately, RTÉ erased the programme to recycle the film.

Ludwig Wittgenstein

Ludwig Wittgenstein (1889–1951), one of the most brilliant and influential philosophers of the twentieth (or, indeed, any) century, spent a considerable amount of time in Ireland and wrote a part of his final work in the country. He visited in 1934, staying in an isolated cottage called 'Rosro' in Connemara. He also lived in Dublin at the Ross Hotel on Parkgate Street near Heuston Station (now the Aisling Hotel) from November 1948 to June 1949. While there he would visit the Botanic Gardens to sit, ruminate and write.

Royal Visits

In total, nine British monarchs have visited Ireland. Most of these came with armies and somewhat combative intentions: Henry II in 1171; King John in 1210; Richard II in 1394; and William III in 1690. George IV was the first king to visit in a non-military capacity, arriving in August, 1821. The remaining royal visits were also undertaken in this spirit with Queen Victoria visiting in 1849 and 1900 and Edward VII making three trips between 1903 and 1907. Elizabeth II arrived a troubled century later in 2011, the first British monarch to visit an independent Ireland.

Queen Victoria's first visit in 1849 took place during the Great Famine. Indeed, Victoria came to be vilified by some as the 'Famine

Queen' in the decades after the tragedy. There was a myth that she had donated a measly £5 to the Famine relief effort but in fact she made a generous donation of £2,000. However, she apparently asked the Sultan of the Ottoman Empire, Abdulmecid I, not to send the £10,000 he wished to donate, as this would upstage her. The Sultan sent £1,000 but also sent three ships with food in secret. The British authorities discovered this and reportedly attempted to block the ships, but they landed in Drogheda.

Victoria's second visit was towards the end of her reign in April 1900. The Queen had sponsored a 'Children's Treat' in the Phoenix Park, attended by 5,000 children. This was an exercise in propaganda, as was her entire visit, which was intended to drum up Irish enlistment to fight in the Boer War. In retaliation, a group of nationalist women led by Maud Gonne, organised the 'Irish Patriotic Children's Treat'. This extraordinary event in June 1900 involved a huge 2-mile long rally of children – possibly 30,000 in the end – parading from Beresford Place to Clonturk Park, waving flags and singing patriotic songs. Along the route, footpaths and

windows were occupied with spectators. Twenty-three vehicles had gone ahead of the children carrying food and drink (20,000 lunches were packed in the days leading up to the event). In the park the children participated in games, the GAA played a demonstration game of hurling and four speakers, including Maud Gonne, delivered speeches. About half a dozen bands were also present to add to the noise. Thus, the largest political rally in Dublin up to that point was largely made up of children. One further result of the Patriotic Children's Treat was that the organising committee and the remaining money left over formed the basis of the establishment of nationalist group Inghinidhe na hÉireann (Daughters of Ireland).

Papal Visits

One pope has visited Ireland: John Paul II in September 1979. He arrived on Saturday 29 September, landing in the flagship Aer Lingus plane, the St Patrick. His first gesture was to bend down and kiss Irish soil (more accurately, the Dublin airport tarmacadam). On a busy three-day trip he visited Dublin, Drogheda,

Clonmacnoise, Galway, Knock, Maynooth and Limerick, flying out of Shannon airport to the USA. He had intended to visit Northern Ireland to say mass at St Patrick's Cathedral in Armagh but security fears prohibited his crossing the border.

More than one million people were said to have turned out to hear the pope say mass in the Phoenix Park on 29 September. If this estimate is correct, that was almost one third of the population of Ireland. A 116ft high steel cross now marks the elevated point where the mass was said. About 200,000 young people heard a Youth Mass at Ballybrit Racecourse, Castlegar, just outside Galway City the following day on 30 September, while about 450,000 turned up to see him at Knock.

An amnesty was agreed for seventy-six prisoners to mark the papal visit. However, Taoiseach Jack Lynch ordered that none of the prisoners be released until after the pope had left owing to the risk of robbery with all of the unattended, empty homes. John Paul was the number one boy's name in 1979.

Blarney Stone
Amongst those who have kissed the Blarney Stone are Winston Churchill, Laurel and Hardy, Billy Connolly and Milston S. Hershey of Hershey's Confectionary.

THE ANIMALS

The Irish are pet-lovers but have a preference for dogs: 35.6 per cent of households in Ireland have one or more pet dogs and 10.4 per cent of households have one or more pet cats. This compares with the United States where 37 per cent have dogs and 32 per cent cats and the United Kingdom where 22 per cent have dogs and 18 per cent have cats. This preference for dogs may well be linked to the country's agrarian roots, where dogs were working animals, and the fact that a relatively greater amount of Irish people live in houses as opposed to apartments.

Robert Cook

Robert Cook (1646?–*c*. 1726) was born in County Waterford and developed into an utter eccentric. He became a vegetarian and wore only linen, refusing wool and leather because of their animal origins, (he was possibly also supporting the family business of textile manufacture). For this he became known as 'Linen Cook'. When a fox attacked his poultry,

it was forced to listen to a dissertation on murder. It was then given a 'sporting chance' at escape, running a gauntlet of farm labourers armed with sticks. In his will he asked to be buried in a linen shroud.

Humanity Martin

Ireland can lay claim to the founder of the RSPCA, Richard Martin (1754–1834). Martin's family owned one of the largest estates in the country and he lived at Ballynahinch Castle in Connemara. As a youth, the hot-headed Martin was prone to duelling, becoming known as 'Hairtrigger Dick'. Most of these duels were fought over the welfare of animals. In 1783 he was seriously wounded in a duel with 'Fighting Fitzgerald', a Mayo landlord who had shot a dog. Believing that all animals had full awareness and feelings, he concluded that abusing or harming them was the same as harming a human being. In 1822 he helped put the world's first animal rights bill through Westminster, which became known as the Martin Act. He then founded the Society for the Prevention of Cruelty to Animals, which became the RSPCA, and he was renamed 'Humanity Martin'.

Dublin Zoo

Dublin Zoo opened in 1831, the third oldest public zoo in the world. The first occupants – forty-six mammals and seventy-two birds – were donated by London Zoo. Cairbre, the roaring MGM studios' lion, was born in Dublin Zoo.

3

CULTURE

LITERATURE AND LIBRARIES

In Ireland, there is a particularly rich literary lineage, from the early Christian scribes, who painstakingly and lovingly committed the word of God to the page, to James Joyce's scribing of the inner world of the twentieth-century individual.

The Book of Kells
One of Ireland's oldest books, and its best known, is the *Book of Kells*; a Latin copy of the Gospels dating from around AD 800. One theory of its journey was that it was begun in St Columba's monastery in Iona, an island off the Scottish coast, but when the Viking raids began in 794 it was moved to the Abbey at Kells where work on the illuminations may have continued. It remained at Kells until 1654, when Cromwell's cavalry arrived and stationed themselves in the town. It was then removed to Dublin and a few years later was presented to Trinity College, Dublin, where it has remained in safekeeping ever since.

There were some additions to the text over the years. Not least, and somewhat unbelievably, there was an attempt to get Queen Victorian and Prince Albert to sign the book. In the event, they only signed a modern flyleaf which was mistakenly believed to be part of the original book. The page with their signatures was removed during a re-binding of the book in 1953.

Understandably, the monks did make some mistakes (they laboured for hours in the scriptorium working only by natural light for fear candles would start a blaze) which pedantic scholars have helpfully made a list of. For instance, where the canonised Bible translates as 'I came not to send peace, but a sword', the *Book of Kells* has transcribed 'I came not [only] to send peace, but joy', which at least has the advantage of sounding less threatening.

An Cathach / The Battler

The *Cathach of Saint Columba* is even older, being a late sixth- or early seventh-century Latin psalter. '*An Cathach*' translates as 'The Battler'. The book got its militaristic name because it came to be used by the O'Donnell clan of Tír Chonaill (mainly present-day Donegal) as a protector before battle. It was customary for a monk or holy man to wear the book, encased in its book shrine, around his neck and walk three times around the O'Donnell troops before battle.

Leabhar na hUidre / Book of the Dun Cow

The oldest surviving manuscript with literature written in the Irish language is the twelfth-century *Book of the Dun Cow* (*Leabhar na hUidre*, in Irish), which was written in Clonmacnoise monastery on the banks of the River Shannon. Legend has it that St Ciarán went to Clonard to study with St Finian, bringing with him a cow which bestowed milk very generously. After the cow died, its hide was kept as a relic and used to create the writing material for the book.

The *Book of the Dun Cow* is a collection of history and legend alongside religious texts, including a partial text of the long tale, the *Táin Bó Cuailgne* (the Cattle Raid of Cooley). The book came to the O'Donnell clan of Donegal. In 1359 a number of the O'Donnell's were kidnapped by the O'Connor family of Sligo. The prisoners were ransomed for the *Book of Dun Cow* and *Leabhar Gearr* (now lost), demonstrating how valuable books were in that period.

BANNED BOOKS

One day during my time as a librarian a young man asked to see me. He wanted to complain of an indecent book. I asked him what was indecent about it, and he said there was a dirty word in it. I asked where and he replied promptly 'Page 164'. Obviously page 164 had printed itself indelibly on his brain. I read the page and asked 'Which word?' He said 'That word' and he pointed to the word 'navel'.

Frank O'Connor, 1962

Ireland has a distinguished history in the censorship of literature. Prior to the nineteenth century there were attempts to control the printing press, focused mainly on politically seditious material, but there was no outright censorship legislation. From the mid-nineteenth century, several censorship acts were passed as the focus turned to obscene literature.

Post-independence in 1922, the Irish governments took censorship into their own hands, with apparent gusto. The weapons used to defend against moral corruption by literature was the Censorship of Publications Act, 1929 and the Censorship of Publications Board, who were there to read and rate any potentially offensive literature.

Publications deemed indecent, that encouraged crime or that promoted the contraception or abortion, were banned. A 1967 act limited the period of prohibition orders on publications to twelve years (though they could, of course, be re-banned). In 1979, the clause on contraception, but not abortion, was withdrawn. Since 1998, no publications have been banned and as such in 2010, after the twelve years had expired, it was declared that no books were censored in Ireland.

Amongst the list of books banned in Ireland at some point were *Catcher in the Rye* and *Brave New World*. Many of these books were banned for their sexual content, reflecting an age of Catholic moral stringency imposed by both Church and State. Edna O'Brien's *The Lonely Girl* was banned after the Archbishop of Dublin, John Charles McQuaid complained personally to Justice Minister Charles Haughey that it was 'particularly bad'.

Strictly speaking James Joyce's *Ulysses* was never banned but only because it was never imported or offered for sale.

WRITERS ON A TREE

Upon the brimming water among the stones
Are nine and fifty swans.

W.B. Yeats, 'The Wild Swans at Coole'

The autograph tree in Coole Park, County Galway, stands as a memorial to the Irish literary revival of the late nineteenth century. Coole was the home of Lady Augusta Gregory who, along with W.B. Yeats, Edward Martyn and George Moore, founded the Abbey Theatre in 1899. Coole was a retreat and social focal point for many of the great writers of the period. The extraordinary copper beech is initialled by George Bernard Shaw, John Masefield, Douglas Hyde, Yeats, Lady Gregory, Sean O'Casey, John Millington Synge, George Russell (AE) and George Moore.

NOBEL PRIZES

Dublin is the only city in the world to have produced three Nobel prize-winners for Literature: W.B. Yeats (1923), George Bernard Shaw (1925) and Samuel Beckett (1969).

LIBRARIES

The song that shakes my feathers
Will thong the leather of your satchel.

Austin Clarke, 'The Blackbird of Derrycairn'

Ireland's first libraries were in the monasteries of the sixth to ninth centuries. Aside from Holy Scripture, these early libraries included Irish literature, canon law and scientific works. The seventh-century poem '*Hisperica Famina*' ('Western Sayings') describes how books were stored not on shelves, but in satchels hung on pegs or racks on the library walls.

The first academic library was established in Trinity College, Dublin in 1592. Since 1801, with the passing of the Act of Union, Trinity has served as a copyright or legal deposit library for the United Kingdom. It is one of only six legal deposit libraries in the UK, meaning it is entitled to receive a copy of every work published in Great Britain. It is also an Irish copyright library. Incidentally, so is the British Library in London.

The first public library in Ireland was Marsh's Library in Dublin, established in 1701 by Narcissus Marsh (1638–1713). While provost of Trinity College, Marsh was unhappy with the restrictions on students' use of the college library – they had to be accompanied by either the Provost or a fellow – so he opened a public library on a site near St Patrick's Cathedral.

Dundalk was the first town to open a municipal public library in 1858, following the Public Libraries Act, 1855. The Public Libraries (Ireland) Act 1902 allowed rural districts and small towns to open public libraries. The American philanthropist Andrew Carnegie (of Carnegie Hall) provided financial support for the building of eighty libraries by local authorities in 1913, many of which are still in operation.

The National Library of Ireland was established under the Dublin Science and Art Museum Act of 1877 and opened in 1890. It was the first library in Europe to adopt the Dewey Decimal classification system.

LANGUAGE

Irish

> The words are the image of the minde, so as they proceeding
> from the minde, the minde must needes be affected with
> the words. So that the speach being Irish, the heart must
> needes bee Irish: for out of the abundance of the heart the
> tongue speaketh.

> Edmund Spencer, *A View of the State of Ireland*, 1633

By the first centuries of the Christian era, the inhabitants of Ireland
were speaking an early form of Irish. This made its way to Scotland
and continued contact ensured that the Scottish and Irish versions of
the language were mutually intelligible until the thirteenth century.

Christian missionaries brought Latin to Ireland in the fifth
century, which became the language of the liturgy. The Viking
settlers of the ninth and tenth centuries brought Norse. They had
learned Gaelic within a few generations, though they contributed
some Norse words. The Anglo-Normans introduced English,
although some of the nobility may have spoken French.

The English colony was weakened in the fourteenth and
fifteenth centuries during the Gaelic Revival and English
disappeared from much of Ireland, being confined to the Pale,
the larger towns and south Wexford. As late as 1515 many of
the nobility (Gaelic or Old English) knew no English. The Tudor
conquest changed this pattern and English was reintroduced,
though Irish remained the language of the majority until
about 1745, when it began its slow decline, helped along by
education and emigration.

Daniel O'Connell, though a native speaker, was famously
dismissive of tongues, stating in 1833:

> I am sufficiently utilitarian not to regret its gradual
> abandonment. A diversity of languages is no benefit ...
> It would be of vast advantage to mankind if all the

inhabitants of the earth spoke the same language. Therefore, although the Irish language is connected with many recollections that twine around the hearts of Irishmen, yet the superior utility of the English tongue, as the medium of modern communication, is so great, that I can witness without sigh the gradual disuse of the Irish.

In the national schools of the nineteenth century some teachers introduced the '*bata scoir*' or 'tally stick'. This was worn by children around their necks. Every time they used Irish, a notch was recorded and at the end of the day they were punished according to how many notches they had incurred.

The Queen's Irish

Queen Elizabeth I expressed an interest in learning Irish and commissioned an Anglo-Irish scholar to produce an Irish language 'primer' for her. The primer – a kind of teaching aid – was handwritten and bound as a one-off manuscript for the queen's own private use. It is assumed that the primer was

produced in the 1560s which was the same time that Elizabeth had ordered funds for a fount of Gaelic type to enable the printing of the New Testament in Irish. She had also expressed concern that any bishops appointed to Ireland should be able to preach in the native tongue. So her interest in Irish was probably not a sudden fascination with linguistics but rather a concern with converting the native Irish to Protestantism through the vernacular.

Fingalian

Fingalian is an extinct English dialect that was spoken by the people of Fingal in north Dublin. It was a kind of spin-off of the Middle English brought to Ireland by the Anglo-Normans. Though it had died out by the nineteenth century there are three remaining examples of Fingalian. However, these are anonymous, humorous poems thought to have been parodies of Fingalian. Here is a taste from *The Fingalian Dance* (*c.* 1650):

> On a day in the Spring,
> As I went to bolring
> to view the jolly Daunciers,
> They did trip it so high
> (Be me shole!) I did spee ...

'Bolring' was the bullring, 'daunciers' were dancers, and it will not do to mention what he spied.

Yola

Fingalian was thought to be similar to the Yola language spoken in Wexford, which again was a dialect that developed down a side track off the thoroughfare of Middle English. Many Irish words made their way into Yola, along with some French borrowings. It was spoken in south county Wexford until the early to mid-nineteenth century. '*Oan, twye/twyne, dhree, voure, veeve, zeese, zeven, ayght, neen, dhen*': it might be guessed what these words are. Other words are less obvious. A Quaker famer called Jacob Poole collected vocabulary. 'Who' was '*fho*', 'what' was '*fade*', 'when' was '*fan*', 'where?' was '*fidi*' and 'why' was '*farthoo*'. 'How' was plain old 'how'.

The first lines of this Yola song, '*Fade teil thee zo lournagh, co Joane, zo knaggee? Th' weithest all curcagh, wafur, an cornee*', translates roughly as, 'What ails you so melancholy, quoth John, so cross? You seem all snappish, uneasy, and fretful'.

The Lord Lieutenant received an address in Yola in 1836 on a visit to Wexford, which was reprinted in a newspaper in 1860:

> *Wee, Vassalès o' 'His Most Gracious majesty', Wilyame ee Vourthe, an, az wee verilie chote, na coshe and loyale dwellerès na Baronie Forthe, crave na dicke luckie acte t'uck neicher th' Eccellencie, an na plaine grabe o' oure yola talke, wi vengem o' core t'gie ours zense o' y gradès whilke be ee-dighte wi yer name …*

Which translates as:

> We, the subjects of his Most Gracious Majesty, William IV, and, as we verily believe, both faithful and loyal inhabitants of the Barony of Forth, beg leave at this favourable opportunity to approach your Excellency, and in the simple dress of our old dialect to pour forth from the strength (or fullness) of our hearts, our sense (or admiration) of the qualities which characterise your name …

WORDS

The Irish have, by all accounts, a way with words. This might be taken to mean they have a facility for the imaginative manipulation of words. But Irish men and women have also come up with entirely new words and phrases. Amongst them:

Bob's Your Uncle
The phrase came into existence after the promotion of Arthur Balfour as Chief Secretary for Ireland. Balfour was somewhat unqualified for the role and it seems that his being the nephew of the Prime Minister Robert Gascoyne-Cecil may have helped

in his elevation to the post. Thus the joke started that if Bob was your uncle a thing was as good as done.

Boycott

This entered the lexicon in 1880 during the Irish Land War owing to a Captain Charles Boycott. Boycott was the land agent of an absentee landlord, Lord Erne. While Parnell had proposed that a tactic of social ostracism might be used against individuals who took on the farms of evicted tenants, it was used against Boycott, the land agent, who was attempting to evict tenants and was thereby complicit in the cruelty of the landlord. Boycott's workers refused to work for him, local businesses refused to trade with him and the postman refused to deliver his mail. Boycott was thus boycotted.

Chance Your Arm

In 1492, during a dispute with the Earl of Kildare, the Earl of Ormonde took refuge in the chapter house at St Patrick's Cathedral in Dublin. Kildare cut a hole through the door and

thrust in his arm, in a gesture of peace and reconciliation. Given the possibility that Ormonde might have cut it off, it was a literal chance of the arm. The risk came good and peace was made.

Entrepreneur

Evidently this is a French word, but its first recorded usage was in a work by a Kerryman, Richard Cantillon. A scion of a Hiberno-Norman landowning family who had fought with James II and after his defeat by William III been dispossessed of their land, he moved to France in his early to mid-twenties. His *Essai sur la Nature du Commerce en Général*, published after his death in 1755, is seen as the first attempt at systematic theorising in the field of economics and was the first exposition of the role played by entrepreneurship in the economy. Entrepreneurs are portrayed as business adventurers; speculators who face the risk of uncertain returns because of the unpredictability of consumer demand. They introduce competition into the market and, in doing this, bring production and prices into line with demand.

Lynching

The story has it that the Mayor of Galway, James Lynch Fitzstephen, executed his own son, Walter in 1493. There are two versions of the story. Walter, returning from a trading expedition to Spain, had thrown a Spanish sailor overboard, apparently in an attempt to conceal the embezzlement of some of his father's money. The other story involves Walter killing an apparent Spanish rival who was seen flirting with his sweetheart. At any rate, the mayor condemned his son to death. Determined to make an example of him in the name of justice, the mayor apparently refused pleas for a reprieve. On the designated morning, a large crowd blocked the way to the execution site, attempting to prevent the hanging. Lynch turned back and entered his own house on Market Street. He climbed to a high window and hanged his son from it. A commemorative structure known as 'Lynch's Window' was erected in 1854 along the side of St Nicholas' Cathedral to commemorate the grisly occasion. This sorry episode may be the origins of the phrase 'Lynch Law' or 'lynching', meaning law administered by a private person, resulting in summary execution. Over time, it evolved to mean mob law.

Phoney

This comes from the Irish word for ring, '*fáinne*'. In the eighteenth century some Irish gold was not considered genuine, and by the early nineteenth-century gold rings from Ireland were known in England as 'fawney'; which became slang for fake. During the 1920s American confidence tricksters traded in fake gold rings also known as 'fawney' which, in an American accent, becomes 'phoney'.

Tory

This was originally used to refer to an Irish outlaw and probably derived from the Irish word '*tóir*', to pursue. Some of these highwaymen and brigands were dispossessed Irish gentry who supported the older, traditional Gaelic order. As such, the word 'Tory' came to refer to a person who wants to conserve the past; the political state of conservatism.

MUSIC

Handel

On the invitation of the Lord Lieutenant, George Frideric Handel came to Dublin to give a series of concerts in 1741 and 1742. In total he stayed for nine months and seemed to enjoy his time in Ireland and the break from his London critics, writing in one letter 'I cannot sufficiently express the kind treatment I receive here'. It is not clear whether Handel had intended for this to happen or not; but Dublin became the first place in the world to hear the *Messiah*. It was performed on 13 April 1742 in Neal's Music Hall, Fishamble Street. In order to accommodate as many people as possible, gentlemen were asked to remove their swords and ladies were requested not to wear hoops in their dresses. Three charities benefited from the performance: Prisoners' Debt Relief, the Mercer's Hospital and the Charitable Infirmary. So moved was a Revd Delaney at the contralto Susanna Cibber's delivery of the line 'he was despised', that he leapt to his feet crying 'Woman, for this be all thy sins forgiven thee!' Whether

this was a reference to a scandalous divorce suit Cibber was involved in or simply an uncontrolled cry of enthusiasm is not known. A second performance took place on 3 June, proceeds going to Handel this time; arguably a deserved reward for having given Dublin this great premiere.

Hymns

The composer of 'All Things Bright and Beautiful' was an Irishwoman, Cecil Frances Alexander (1818–1895). She was born in Eccles Street, Dublin and moved with her family to Wicklow and then Tyrone. She married William Alexander, a Tyrone rector who went on to become Church of Ireland Bishop of Derry and Raphoe. She also wrote 'Once in Royal David's City' and 'Legend of Stumpie's Brae', a ballad in Ulster-Scots dialect. Her *Hymns for Little Children* ran to at least sixty-nine, possibly closer to 100, editions.

Buncrana, County Donegal, has laid claim to its part in the composition of the hymn 'Amazing Grace', though it is admittedly one of the more tenuous links between a place and a song. John Newton (1725–1807) was working in the African slave trade when, on 21 March 1748, during a voyage home to England, his ship was hit by a violent Atlantic storm and he uttered his first prayer for mercy. The ship survived the storm and he came onto land in one piece on the shores of Lough Swilly. This, he later claimed, was the first moment of his conversion story; 'The hour I first believed'. It was another six months before he could cast off sin and even after that he continued slave trading. Forced to leave the maritime trade after a fit in 1854, he began to concentrate on his faith, becoming a Calvinist and eventually a clergyman. He turned against the slave trade, expressing deep regrets in later life and supporting William Wilberforce's abolition campaign, penning the abolitionist tract *Thoughts upon the African Slave Trade* (1787). 'Amazing Grace' was not written until after 1771 and was published in *Olney Hymns*, a collaborative volume with the poet William Cowper in 1779.

ARCHITECTURE AND BUILDINGS

Buildings and Structures

The current Bank of Ireland building on College Green, completed in 1739, was the first purpose-built parliament building in Europe. It was sold to the Bank of Ireland in 1800 after the Act of Union dissolved the Irish parliament.

Leinster House, now home to the houses of the Oireachtas, was once the private residence of the Duke of Leinster. Built in 1745, it was the largest private house in Dublin.

Carlow Castle is thought to have been built in the early thirteenth century. It withstood attacks in 1494 and 1641. It did not, however, survive the remodelling efforts of a local physician called Middleton who leased the castle in 1814, to have it converted into a lunatic asylum. In his effort to demolish the interior, the explosions instead successfully destroyed all but one wall and its towers.

Sometimes castles are deliberately destroyed by their owners. Athlumney Castle, outside Navan, was burnt down twice by its owners. In 1649 it was set alight to prevent its falling into the hands of Cromwell's troops, and in 1690 it was set ablaze to prevent its being taken by William of Orange. It has remained a ruin since this second fire.

Lynch's Castle is situated on the main street in Galway, Shop Street. Build around the beginning of the sixteenth century; it was once the seat of the powerful Lynch family, one of the fourteen tribes of Galway. Today it is the branch of a bank and is the oldest building in everyday commercial use in the country.

Mellows Bridge, built in 1764, is the oldest bridge in Dublin city still in use. Originally called Queen's Bridge, it became Queen Maeve Bridge in 1923 before becoming Mellows Bridge after the republican leader Liam Mellows, who was executed during the Civil War in 1922.

Ireland's oldest bridge was uncovered by archaeologists in 1996. It dates from 804 and led to the monastic settlement of Clonmacnoise. At 553ft long and 17ft across it demonstrated how important Clonmacnoise was as an economic, political and religious centre.

Nelson's Pillar

Nelson's Pillar was a 121ft high granite pillar on O'Connell Street, built in 1808–09 and carrying a 13ft statue of Horatio Nelson. Many in independent Ireland were opposed to this huge monument to a famous British navyman. However, despite the issue coming up for debate over the years, no conclusion as to its future was ever reached. On 8 March 1966, a group of former IRA men decided to reach a decision for everybody and planted a bomb that destroyed the upper part of the pillar. Their leader, Joe Christie, was a socialist revolutionary who had been dismissed from the IRA ten years previously. The timing was apparently meant to coincide with the 50th anniversary of the 1916 Rising. Thankfully, nobody was hurt by the explosion. In fact, the real damage was yet to come. On 14 March, Irish army engineers were employed to destroy the

remainder of the pillar. This planned detonation did more damage than the original, blasting out many windows on O'Connell Street.

Nelson's last stand had some footnotes, however. Seven enterprising students from the National College of Art and Design stole his head on St Patrick's Day as a fundraising prank to pay off some Student Union debts. They leased the head to an antique dealer in London to put in his shop window for the sum of £200 a month. The head also appeared in a commercial for ladies' stockings and made a guest appearance on stage at the Olympia with The Dubliners. The head was eventually presented to the Lady Nelson of the day about half a year after it was stolen. It is currently in the Gilbert Library on Pearse Street.

Architects

The architect who designed the White House was one James Hoban (*c.* 1762–1831) from Callan, County Kilkenny. He worked on the Royal Exchange and the Custom House in Dublin before emigrating to the United States. He met President Washington in Philadelphia in 1792, and decided to enter a competition to design public buildings. He won the contest to design the President's house, beating an anonymous submission by Thomas Jefferson in the process. The building showed the influence of Leinster House.

His White House was burned by the British in 1814 but was reconstructed, with Hoban's involvement, and completed in 1829.

Many of Dublin's finest public buildings were designed by James Gandon (1742–1823). Gandon was born in London and in 1780 was chosen to design the new Custom House. He also designed the Four Courts, O'Connell Bridge and King's Inn (this was completed by his pupil Henry Aaron Baker) and extended the building that is now the Bank of Ireland on College Green. Despite his achievements, or perhaps because of this monopoly on public commissions, Gandon attracted much resentment. The nasty *Letters addressed to parliament, and to the public in general*, on various improvements of the metropolis (1786) were the worst expression of this resentment.

Follies

The 'Jealous Wall' at Belvedere House in County Westmeath is Ireland's largest and most spectacular folly.

Belvedere House was built by Robert Rochfort. Known as 'The Wicked Earl' for reasons that will become apparent, his seat was at Gaulston Park in nearby Rochfortbridge. When he discovered that his young wife was having an affair with his brother, Arthur, he ran the latter out of Ireland and imprisoned the former at Gaulston. There she was forbidden to see anyone other than elderly servants and was even barred from seeing her children. She remained imprisoned for thirty-one years. In the meantime, Robert lived as a bachelor, rose through the ranks of society and built Belvedere in 1740. Here he quarrelled with his other brother, George, who lived across the fields at Rochfort House. Rochfort House was larger and grander than Belvedere and Robert's solution was to erect an enormous sham ruin to block the infuriating view.

NATIONAL EMBLEMS

The Tricolour

The tricolour became the official national flag in 1937. It was first flown not on top of some civic building in Dublin as one might expect, but in Waterford. The flag was created by a Waterford native John Francis Meagher, who first flew it in his hometown on 7 March 1848. A member of Young Ireland, Meagher created a symbol of peace between Ireland's warring tribes: the green representing the Irish Volunteers, the orange the Orange Order and the white, of course, representing peace between the two. Meagher took part in the Young Ireland rebellion in that same year of 1848 and for this crime of high treason was exiled to the antipodes, never setting foot in his home country again. The tricolour was flown in 1916.

The Union Jack was flown for the first time from Dublin Castle on 1 January 1801, the day the Act of Union came into force.

National Anthem

'A Soldier's Song' or '*Amhrán na bhFiann*' was officially recognised as the national anthem in 1926. De Valera denied that his choice of Fianna Fáil as the name for his new political party, founded in the same year of 1926, had anything to do with its appearance in the opening line of the new anthem. It was written in 1908 by Peadar Kearney, a Dublin house-painter, poet and writer, who was a member of the Gaelic League, Irish Republican Brotherhood and Oliver Bond 1798 Club. It was for this latter club that he and his childhood friend Patrick Heaney wrote the song – Heaney the music, Kearney the lyrics – with Kearney noting afterwards that they wrote it 'in order to impress on Irishmen that they did not have to join the British army to be soldiers'. An Irish version was translated by Liam Ó Rinn. It was only after it was sung in the GPO during the 1916 Rising, and afterwards in various internment camps, that it assumed its position as the unofficial anthem, replacing God Save Ireland in this regard. In 1934, the Department of Finance acquired copyright from Kearney. The State does not hold the copyright to any Irish version, meaning that unlike Kearney's and Heaney's estates, Ó Rinn's estate never received any royalties.

4

SPORTS
AND LEISURE

IRELAND AT THE OLYMPICS

Martin Sheridan

With nine medals, Martin Sheridan, is Ireland's most successful Olympian. Unfortunately, he did not compete for Ireland. Sheridan was born in Bohola in County Mayo and emigrated to the United States at the age of eighteen. He served with the NYPD where he competed for the Irish American Athletic Club. As if to confirm his status as an incorrigible Irishman, his brother married one of Michael Collins' sisters.

Competing at the St Louis Games in 1904 he won a gold medal for the discus throw. Four years later in London he won two gold medals for the discus throw and the discus throw Greek style and a bronze medal for the standing long jump. In between, he competed at the Intercalated Olympic Games in Athens in 1906. There he produced an incredible all-round performance, winning gold medals in the discus throw and shot putt as well as silver medals in the standing long jump, standing high jump and stone throw. After the 1906 Athens Games he was presented with a long vault by the King of Greece to mark his being the finest competitor of those Games. He brought this home to Ireland and it is now displayed on the wall of the Community Centre in Bohola.

Sheridan sadly died very prematurely in 1918, the day before his thirty-seventh birthday, an early victim of the Spanish Flu pandemic. His obituary in the *New York Times* described him as 'one of the greatest athletes [the United States] has ever known'.

Ireland's First Gold

Before the 1906 Intercalated Games, National Olympic Committees generally did not exist and athletes could enter themselves independently. John Pius Boland, of Dublin, went to the first Olympic Games in Athens in 1896 as a spectator but ended up entering the tennis tournament and winning the men's singles and doubles (with a German partner). He thus became Ireland's first Olympic gold medallist (although technically prior to 1904 the winners received silver medals and the runners-up bronze). There was no Irish flag to raise at the medal ceremony. Boland remarked that they should have had a flag with a gold harp on a green background, but as there was no time to source one, the Union Jack was raised.

Tom Kiely

This issue of independent enrolment was a point of particular importance to Tom Kiely, the Tipperary man who won the 'all round' athletics competition at the 1904 Games. Kiely had refused to accept funding from either the English Amateur Athletic Association or the New York Athletic Club to pay his fare and compete for them, instead raising the necessary funds in Tipperary and Waterford in order to travel independently, insisting that he would represent only Ireland.

Athens, 1906

Three athletes competing at the 1906 Intercalated Games in Athens – Peter O'Connor, Con Leahy and John Daly – were entered for the competition by the Irish Amateur Athletic Association and the Gaelic Athletic Association (GAA). They were provided with green blazers, caps with a gold shamrock and an Irish flag embossed with a harp bearing the inscription '*Erin Go Brach*'. However, as the rules of the Games changed to allow nomination by National Olympic Committees only, and as Ireland did not have an Olympic Committee, these three were entered by the British Olympic Association and found on registering for the Games that they were competing for the United Kingdom team.

Peter O'Connor won the silver medal for the long jump (he claimed a victory was sabotaged as a result of his insistence that he was competing for Ireland). During the medal ceremony, O'Connor, seeing the Union Jack being raised, climbed the flagpole in the middle of the field to a height of about 20ft and waved his Irish flag. Two fellow Irish athletes and some sympathetic American team members stood guard at the base of the flagpole and prevented the officials stopping his demonstration. All this took place in front of Greek and British royalty.

Olympic Rebels
Two former Olympic cyclists took part in the Easter Rising. Brothers Michael and John Walker had competed for Ireland in the 1912 Stockholm Olympics in the 200-mile road race. No doubt this training came in handy during the Rising when bicycles were used by despatch riders to courier messages as well as being 'hit and run' vehicles.

Olympic Women
The first Irish female Olympic medallist was Beatrice Geraldine Hill-Lowe, who took a bronze medal for archery at the 1908 Games. At the time this was the only sport open to women as they were only allowed to compete in sports fully clothed.

Ireland's first female competitors post-independence were tennis players Phoebe Blait White and Hilda Wallis in 1924.

Ireland's first female competitor in athletics was Maeve Kyle who ran in the 1956 Melbourne Games in the 100m and 200m races, defying a letter to the *Irish Times* that stated 'A sports field is no place for a woman' and decried the selection of a female athlete for the Irish team as 'most unbecoming, unseemly and degrading of womenfolk'.

Olympic Firsts

The first team representing Ireland at the Summer Olympic Games competed in 1924.

Ireland's first Winter Olympic Games Team competed in 1992.

Ireland's first Olympic medal as an independent nation was a gold medal, won by Pat O'Callaghan at the 1928 Amsterdam Games for the Men's hammer throw.

Ireland's first medals in the art competitions came in 1924 when Jack B. Yeats won a silver medal for mixed painting and Oliver St John Gogarty won a bronze for mixed literature.

Dublin's first bid to host the Olympics was in 1936. The second, and most recent, bid came in 1940.

THE GAELIC ATHLETIC ASSOCIATION (GAA)

The GAA grew from inauspicious beginnings. The inaugural meeting was held on 1 November 1884 in the billiards room of Hayes Commercial and Family Hotel, Thurles. Seven men attended. Maurice Davin was elected president of the Gaelic Athletic Association for the Preservation and Cultivation of National Pastimes. Michael Cusack, John Wyse Power and John McKay were elected secretaries. Within three years of its foundation an all-Ireland competition was held in both football and hurling.

The GAA had a famous ban, so famous it was simply known as 'The Ban', which prohibited GAA members from taking part in 'foreign games' like rugby, soccer or hockey. The Ban, technically Rule 27, was introduced in 1902 and remained in force until 1971. It was policed by 'Vigilance Committees' who would attend these 'imported games' and report on any GAA players caught betraying their nation with a rugby ball. Even watching these sports was not allowed. If caught, players were liable to incur a lengthy suspension. In 1938, Douglas Hyde, then the President of Ireland, was removed as a patron of the organisation for attending an international soccer match in Dalymount Park, Dublin.

Lest anybody doubt the deep commitment of GAA fans there is a story from Cavan town in 1925. Cavan were playing Kerry in the football semi-final in Tralee. There were no radios in Cavan in those days. There were two telephone lines, in the post office and the Garda barracks, but all calls were routed through Dublin and a legacy of the recent civil war meant that there was no communication between Tralee and Dublin and, *ergo*, none between Tralee and Cavan. Local initiative prevailed, however. The chemist was a keen keeper of carrier pigeons. He and a friend drove the eight hours to Tralee in his baby Ford to with two of his pigeons. On Sunday evening a large crowd had gathered outside the chemist's house and the pigeons arrived, both carrying the sad news that Cavan had lost by one point.

Caid

Caid was a traditional type of football particularly popular in rural areas like the Dingle Peninsula in Kerry. One version of the game contained itself to a field, the aim being to put the ball through goals. A second version was a less orderly affair involving teams of unlimited numbers often from two neighbouring parishes. The ball was tossed up between them at an agreed central point and most of the daylight hours that Sunday would be spent trying to get the ball 'home' to the parish over fields and hedges. It was very much a contact sport: scrimmages, tripping, pushing and wrestling were components.

Soccer

Ireland played its first international soccer match in 1882 against England, and lost 13-0. At the time, the organising body was the Irish Football Association, based in Belfast. After partition in 1921, the Football Association of Ireland was established as a rival organisation.

Hurling

Hurling has a very long history in Ireland, possibly extending back 2,000 years. Brehon law is thought to have recognised the sport and it is mentioned in twelfth-century manuscripts.

In the eighteenth century there were two versions of the sport played. In the northern part of the country it was like field hockey or shinty; no handling of the ball was allowed, the stick was narrow and crooked and a hard wooden ball was used. It was called *camán*, anglicised to 'commons'. In the southern counties the sport was called *iomán* or *báire* and was much more akin to the current game: the ball could be handled and carried on the stick, the stick was flat and round-headed and the sliothar was soft and made of animal hair. This southern variant was patronised by the gentry as a spectator and gambling pastime and it was associated with fairs and other public gatherings.

In the nineteenth century increased sectarian tensions and changes in gentry lifestyle diminished this patronage and the sport declined amongst the peasantry along with other traditional amusements. It was revived by the GAA. By 1913 the rules had been rewritten and it spread rapidly from Dublin.

FAIRS

Beidh aonach amárach i gContae an Chláir
Cén mhaith dom é, ní bheidh mé ann?

Traditional

Puck Fair

The Puck Fair in Killorglin is said to be Ireland's oldest fair, although there is no way of dating its origins accurately. Certainly there was a charter from James I in 1603 which granted legal status to the fair. It is currently held for three days, staring on 10 August, and has evolved into a mixture of market and street festival. The fair's most noteworthy aspect, and the aspect from which it gets its name, is the crowning of 'King Puck', a wild he-goat, by 'Queen Puck', usually a local schoolgirl. After his coronation, the king is put in a cage on a high stand in the middle of the town square and the festivities can begin.

There are various explanations as to the origins of King Puck from a daring Paul-Revere-style run by a 'puck' from the mountains to Killorglin warning the inhabitants of the arrival of Cromwell's pillaging men to a brave puck who faced down a band of Norsemen and sent them fleeing back to their ship.

Donnybrook Fair

Donnybrook Fair was held annually for over six centuries. It was established under charter in 1204 and had its heyday in the eighteenth century. Lasting a week or two and held in August, there was the usual dealing in goods associated with fairs along with a lot of drunkenness and disorder. The term 'a donnybrook' made its way into the lexicon to denote a riot, brawl or scene of an uproar. The disorderly behaviour led to a campaign for its suppression, led by the Committee for the Abolition of Donnybrook Fair, and it was scrapped in 1855.

World Fair

The World Fair was held in Dublin in 1907 and was also known as the Irish International Exhibition. An international exhibition had previously been undertaken by the Royal Dublin Society in 1849. These events were part trade fair, part industrial showcase and part entertainment.

It is estimated that 2.75 million people attended between May and November. The fair involved a huge undertaking of building works on an area of 52 acres in between Donnybrook and Ballsbridge. The architectural centrepiece was the Central Palace, rising 150ft and covering 2.5 acres. Other features included the Palace of Industries, the Palace of Fine Arts, the Palace of Mechanical Arts and the Grand Concert Hall, which seated 2,000 people. There was also the Water Chute, a 90ft high slide from which people were launched in boats into a pond below. The most popular attraction was a recreated Somali village, part of a display called 'Life in British Somaliland', in which native Somalis demonstrated how they made their native crafts, tools and clothes and sold some of the produce to visitors.

The buildings were sold off piecemeal in the 18 months after the exhibition ended and Herbert Park was built on 32 of the acres. The only remaining construction from 1907 is the pond.

ST PATRICK'S DAY

St Patrick's Day is a public holiday in two places outside of Ireland: Newfoundland and Labrador in Canada and the Caribbean island of Montserrat. Although currently a British

Overseas Territory, a census in 1678 revealed that 70 per cent of Montserrat's population was Irish. The Irish population had dropped to under 650 by 1729, though it is surmised that many Irish married and had families with women who were former slaves. Slavery ended on the island in 1824. To this day, visitors' passports are decorated with a shamrock-shaped stamp when entering Montserrat and the national dress is green, white and gold. You will find a Kinsale and Galway on the island, and possibly meet Reillys, O'Briens and Kellys.

The first St Patrick's Day parade took place outside Ireland, in Boston, Massachusetts, in 1737.

ELECTIONS

Elections have something of the fair day celebration about them. Johann Friedrich Hering, a German traveller to Ireland, was in Balinrobe for a general election in late 1806. The electors and voters flocking into the town gave rise 'to much revelry and brawling'. The entire town was covered in handbills advertising the various candidates. Elections went on for days and he notes that each day the polling-house was full of voters, whose votes were written down and who expressed their opinions publicly. 'The curious were not wanting either, and this colourful exchange gave us foreigners some entertainment'. When the votes were counted the two newly elected members were carried all around the streets on big arm-chairs amongst the cheering crowd, with the new MPs tossing gold and silver coins to their admirers!

5

FOOD
AND DRINK

Moderation, we find, is an extremely difficult thing to get
in this country.

Flann O'Brien

HISTORY OF DRINKING

The main beverages in medieval Ireland, aside from milk, appear
to have been ale, beer and mead. Wine, which was imported, was
drunk amongst the ruling classes.

Whiskey was probably not introduced in Ireland until the
fourteenth century. The word whiskey comes from the Irish
'*uisge beatha*' or 'water of life'. This may have been a loan
translation of the Latin '*aqua vitae*' which was used to denote
intoxicating drink from the fourteenth century.

Initially, whiskey was largely used for medicinal purposes,
mixed as it was with herbs and spices. From the sixteenth
century, however, the authorities were expressing concern over
the amount of whiskey being consumed.

There were a number of reasons for attempts to control the
production, sale and distribution of alcohol from this period.
Taxes on alcohol offered a significant source of revenue in
an otherwise undeveloped economy. The government were
also concerned to regulate consumption of grain, making

sure it could be channelled into food production during times of scarcity. Finally, whiskey was seen as providing comfort to Irish rebels while public houses were seen as refuges and meetings places.

Public houses were generally confined to towns in medieval and early modern Ireland, meaning that regular alcohol consumption was a feature of urban life. In rural areas, consumption tended to be less regular and associated with special occasions. It was associated with hospitality, for instance, and visitors were always offered a drink. Drinking also took place on special occasions: weddings, wakes, fairs and markets and traditional religious festivals. The regular beverage of rural people was milk.

By the eighteenth century spirits became much more readily available and whiskey began to replace wine amongst the upper classes and ale amongst the poorer classes. The government tried to gain control of the distilling industry: raising taxes on whiskey and outlawing small stills. This served only to generate a flourishing illicit alcohol industry. This illicit trade made alcohol consumption in rural areas much more regular.

From the mid-nineteenth century, with the advent of railways, the commercial distilleries and breweries which had been operating in towns for a century began to penetrate the rural market. The sale of spirits was also undercut by major increases in the duty on whiskey in the 1850s. Between 1850s and 1900s per capita consumption of spirits fell by almost half while consumption of beer increased sevenfold. Ireland was becoming a nation of beer drinkers. By 1914 brewing was the largest industry in the country when measured by the value of its output. By the 1970s about one third of alcohol drunk was spirits, 60 per cent was beers and stout and 5 per cent was wine. In 2005 the statistics categories were: 53 per cent beer, 20 per cent wine, 19 per cent spirits, 8 per cent other.

In the first half of the twentieth century drinking was still predominantly a male pastime, being confined to pubs, both urban and rural. The explosion in consumption occurred in the second half of the century; doubling between 1960 and 1980. One reason was the arrival of women at the party. In the 1960s, few women entered pubs and if they did they confined themselves discreetly to snugs. By the 1980s women constituted a new market for publicans, who diversified their products accordingly. Alcohol became more widely available, being offered for sale in off licences and supermarkets, while drinking increasingly took place in the home, in clubs and in restaurants. The traditional model of the man in the pub with his pint was replaced by a mixture of genders and ages accessing alcohol in any number of outlets.

The Irish are not the heaviest consumers of alcohol. The OECD put Ireland tenth out of forty countries in terms of alcohol consumption for 2009, with the United Kingdom just behind in eleventh position (the French consumed the largest amount). Another report recorded that the average Irish adult consumed 11.9 litres of pure alcohol in 2010: the equivalent of 425 pints of lager, 125 bottles of wine or 45 bottles of vodka. Given that 19 per cent of adults are abstainers; that leaves quite a lot for the less abstemious. In short, it would seem that the drinkers are drinking on behalf of the non-drinkers. If one stereotype – that the Irish drink more than anybody else – is undercut, a related one – that the Irish are enthusiastic binge drinkers – is wholeheartedly upheld.

PINTS OF PLAIN

The most famous Irish drink is Guinness. The Guinness story began in 1759, when Arthur Guinness signed a 9,000-year lease on a disused brewery in St James' Gate in Dublin. Marketing geniuses at Guinness recently converted the year into a time – 17.59 – when all and sundry are to raise a toast to Mr Guinness on 'Arthur's Day'; an occasion which, being entirely made up and a living advertisement, shouldn't be popular at all, but has become very popular indeed in the space of a few short years. Only time will tell if the day becomes a national holiday or footnote 78 in *The History of Marketing* (2100).

Initially the brewery produced beer and ale, but by the 1790s was making the porters or stouts that would become synonymous with the brand. By 1833 the brewery was the largest in Ireland; by

1886 it was the largest in the world; and by the 1930s Guinness was among the seven largest companies in the world. Guinness was a very big employer in Dublin and had a reputation as a very good one. During the First World War, Guinness guaranteed to every employee serving in uniform that their jobs would be secure on their return, while they also paid a half salary to the soldier's family. A Guinness employee in the 1920s had access to full medical and dental care, a company-funded pension, subsidised meals and educational benefits, not to mention two daily pints of the product. None of this is surprising given the philanthropic nature of the Guinness dynasty. The original Arthur Guinness founded Ireland's first Sunday school. Benjamin Lee Guinness (1798–1868) financed the restoration of St Patrick's Cathedral. Arthur Guinness (1840–1915) restored the Coombe hospital and landscaped St Stephen's Green which he then gave to the public. Edward Cecil Guinness (1847–1927) contributed almost £1 million to slum clearance and housing projects.

There is a story about Guinness and the writer Brendan Behan. Behan, a famously enthusiastic drinker (he described himself as a drinker with writing problems), was apparently asked by Guinness to come up with a slogan. He agreed and asked for a number of crates of the stuff to be sent to him, presumably as oil to grease his wit. When a Guinness representative called to the house to see him, he found Behan on the floor having made great progress through the contents of the crates. 'I've got it', Behan allegedly announced, 'Guinness makes you drunk'; certainly true and therefore presumably not allowable as an advertising slogan.

In 1984, on a visit to Ireland, US President Ronald Regan stopped off in a Dublin watering hole for a pint of Guinness. He took one sip before leaving, after which secret service agents smashed the glass. Incidentally, the same logic applies to the bowl of Shamrocks given to American Presidents every St Patrick's Day in the White House. It is destroyed immediately since, for security reasons, it is not allowable to give food or floral gifts to US presidents.

POITÍN

Poitín, or poteen to anglicise the spelling, is a word for any kind of Irish moonshine or illicitly produced alcohol. The term is a diminutive of the Irish word 'pota' or pot, as it was distilled in small pot stills. The base ingredient is immaterial: grain, potatoes, sugar, crab apples have all been persuaded to make poitín. Poitín is of eye-watering strength: some could reach 95 per cent alcohol by volume. It was popular at weddings and wakes and sold in great volume around Christmas time. It also had other uses: it was rubbed into the joints as a palliative remedy for arthritis and rheumatism and greyhounds were said to run better after being given a taste. It was made illegal in the seventeenth century but an illicit industry thrived until the Great Famine which decimated both the distillers and the consumers. The Irish constabulary took over the policing of the industry from the 1850s and brought it under government control. Legal production for export was allowed in 1989 and from 1997 it could be sold in its country of origin.

TEMPERANCE

Ireland generated some very successful temperance and total abstinence movements over the years. There had been considerable alarm from the 1790s over the consumption of whiskey and poitín. Inspired by similar movements in the United States, the first substantial temperance societies were established in 1829. The Irish being perhaps prone to extremes, the first truly successful movement came after total abstinence was imported from England. The teetotal crusade of Fr Theobald Mathew, a Cork Capuchin friar, began in 1838 and was an outstanding success with perhaps 5 million people of a total population of 8.2 million taking the teetotal pledge by 1841–42. The reasons for the success are difficult to delineate. Certainly, the cause was supported by the majority of the hierarchy and many priests. However, the mainly rural Catholic pledge-takers were perhaps influenced by the fact that Fr Mathews was endowed with miraculous powers in the popular mind. Mathew was something of a controversial figure within his own church and alienated many clergy for various reasons, including his designation of the pledge as a sacred vow, the mismanagement of finances and, more unforgivably for the time, his friendship with Protestants and acceptance of a government pension. Daniel O'Connell took the pledge, and his Repeal movement made use of various aspects of the movement from temperance reading rooms to the sobriety of the population.

Support dwindled after the Famine but there was a revival of total abstinence when the Pioneer Total Abstinence Association of the Sacred Heart was set up in 1898–1901 by a Jesuit priest, Fr James Cullen. By the 1920s the association had about 300,000 members, rising to 500,000 in the 190s, and it remains one of the largest temperance organisations in the world. Ireland still has as remarkably high abstinence rate, as noted above.

Sunday closing was introduced in the five main Irish cities in 1878 and although this has been revoked, there are still two days a year when alcohol cannot legally be sold in Ireland: Good Friday and Christmas Day. Easter Saturday and St Stephen's Day are amongst the busiest pub days of the year.

OTHER LAWS REGARDING ALCOHOL

As of 2003, it is illegal to reduce the cost of alcohol for limited periods during the day. In other words, 'happy hour' is now illegal.

The law banning the sale of alcohol on Good Friday and Christmas Day were first introduced as part of Intoxicating Liquor Act. The ban also originally included St Patrick's Day.

The one exception to the Good Friday rule came after what became known as the 'Good Friday Disagreement' in 2010. A Celtic League rugby union match between Munster and Leinster was scheduled for Good Friday. Not wanting to lose valuable revenue, the publicans in Limerick went to court and won the right to open their pubs, becoming the first to legally serve alcohol since 1928 on the day.

Trinity College laws state that any student may demand a glass of wine during an exam; provided they are carrying their sword, of course.

HISTORY OF EATING

In Gaelic society, pastoral farming prevailed meaning that the diet centred on the consumption of meat, which was eaten in large quantities, and other animal products like milk and butter. People ate fistfuls of rancid butter rolled in oats and even consumed it on its own. Until the end of the sixteenth century, tillage crops like cereals were seen as a supplement to meat and dairy foods.

During the seventeenth century arable farming expanded and with it the consumption of cereals. The influence of the plantations and English farming ideas are important here: the land was put under the plough and tillage spread gradually. By the end of the century the country was producing a variety of grains, fruits and sweet herbs while fisheries were established along the coasts catching of bass, mullet, eels, hake, herrings, oysters, cockles and mussels.

The settlers had their stomachs turned by some of the dietary habits of the natives. Their penchant for blood, in a jellied form or mixed with butter, oats or salt was disgusting to them. They were also repelled by the habit of eating animal entrails, carrion and horse meat. There was also their drinking of warm milk, straight from the cow, the rancid butter mentioned above, their unhopped ale and their preference for oatcakes over wheaten bread. Changes in taste were a by-product of colonisation.

In Gaelic society food was distributed as tribute or rent payments to lords. As the Gaelic system disappeared, this view of food was replaced with a more commercialised one. Food became a commodity and its consumption was dictated by price and buyer income and preference.

By the eighteenth century the class divisions in food consumption were pronounced. The Irish upper classes were eating like their English counterparts. Luxury products like sugar, tea, coffee and confectionary rose sharply. Meat and bread were still central, as was dairy produce, but cereals, vegetables and fruit were also a part of the diet.

At the lower end of the social scale, diets centred on dairy products supplemented with vegetables and grains. The diet amongst the peasant class was to become much narrower as the century progressed, until by the start of the nineteenth century they were mainly subsisting on potatoes and milk. The quantities consumed were very large: daily estimates range between 10 and 15 pounds of potatoes per adult male. Skimmed milk and buttermilk were the most common beverages. In the 'hungry months' of summer between the end of one potato crop and the beginning of the next harvest, oatmeal and herrings were eaten. It is estimated that the potato had become the staple food of about one third of the population on the eve of the Famine. This dietary dependency on one food was to have disastrous consequences in the years between 1845 and 1850 when widespread failure of the potato crop devastated the poor population.

After the Great Famine, diets became more varied; a result of augmented incomes and living standards which saw increasing amounts of imported foods. The railways brought new items to rural areas as the nineteenth century progressed. Tea replaced milk as the beverage of choice; cheap cuts of meat made weekly appearance at the dinner table as opposed to only at Christmas and Easter. One irony of this increased variety was a decrease in the nutritional quality of the diets of the working class. The simple pre-famine fare of potato and milk was more nourishing that the newer diets of cereals, bread, butter and tea.

As the twentieth century progressed diets became even more varied. The urban-rural and class differences lessened. Today, the potato is still an important component of the Irish diet, as are the dairy products that the population have long demonstrated a fondness for.

TOBACCO

Ireland, though it might sound surprising, was once a tobacco-growing country. As early as 1698 there were calls to introduce tobacco cultivation as a component of Irish economic improvement. In fact, prohibition of tobacco cultivation was extended to Ireland under Charles II. The ban was lifted in the late eighteenth century and by 1831 the plant was being extensively grown in County Wexford, in particular. One theory suggests that Ireland benefitted from the impact of the American Revolution, with relations between this prime producer of tobacco and the United Kingdom remaining unresolved until the treaty of 1818. On one estimate a fifth of all tobacco consumed in the United Kingdom in this period came from Ireland.

A prohibition act specific to Ireland was introduced in 1832, although Daniel O'Connell spoke out against the measure. The de Valera government of the 1930s, as part of a protectionist drive, made the last great effort to revive the crop but its success was its downfall: encouraged by the cash to be made, increasing numbers of farmers sought to introduce the crop leading the government to introduce market control measures. This strict legislation concerning the price paid for tobacco and restrictions on growing permits put an end to the industry.

FINE DINING

Jammet's restaurant was the epitome of high-class food; the aristocracy of gastronomy in Ireland from 1900 to 1967. It was a jarring monument to luxury at a time of incredible poverty and austerity. It was opened by two French brothers – Michel and Francois Jammet – and found a home on Nassau Street from 1926.

John Lennon was one of its most famous visitors. In a characteristic sample of his sharp wit, his note in the visitor's book read: 'The other three are saving up to come here'. Amongst the marble, gilt and crystal many more well-known (and rich) people came to sample the fare including Elizabeth Taylor, Bing Crosby, Walt Disney, Orson Welles, Maureen O'Hara and Noel Coward. The glitterati and the literati both lined their stomachs and wet their whistles. W.B. Yeats had his own table in the restaurant and on 6 March 1933 he apparently dined in the restaurant's Blue Room with fellow writers Brinsley MacNamara, James Stephens, Lennox Robinson, F.R. Higgins, Seamus O'Sullivan, Peadar O'Donnell, Francis Stuart, Frank O'Connor, Miss Somerville, J.M. Hone and Walter Starkie, a conversation that a creative writing student might like to recreate in an idle few moments.

FOOD FACTS

The Irish consume more chocolate than any other nation, ingesting on average a worrying 11 kg per person per year.

The first Turkish delight chocolate was made in a factory in Cobh in the 1890s by the Hadji Bey company.

Never say the Irish have not contributed to culinary history. The flavoured crisp was developed by Joe 'Spud' Murphy and his employee Seamus Burke of Tayto in the 1950s. At the time, crisps came with an attached bag of salt that one sprinkled over the contents. Murphy, an enthusiastic crisp eater, founded Tayto in 1954 and charged Burke with concocting a revolution in crisps. Burke came up with the cheese and onion flavour and they found a way of seasoning the crisps during the manufacturing process.

6

EDUCATION

HEDGE SCHOOLS

The penal laws forbade Catholics from attending universities abroad and from teaching. Violating this latter law carried with it punishments of a £20 fine, three month's imprisonment or

banishment to Barbados. The result was an illegal, unregulated network of schools that have become known as the 'hedge schools'. It must be said that despite their illegality, they were largely ignored by the authorities. There is no record of any school teacher being convicted.

The educational restrictions imposed by the penal laws were repealed in 1782 but the hedge schools persisted into the nineteenth century. The 1824 census suggested that there were approximately 10,000 hedge schools with about 500,000 pupils.

While the image of children receiving their lessons by the side of a hedge offering them protection and cover might have had some truth in summer months, very often schooling took place in structures, albeit primitive ones like mud cabins. The schools were also found in more unlikely places like graveyards, mills, wheat-stores, barns and chapels. Teachers would also teach in homes during the winter months in return for full board. More permanent school structures were constructed, generally after the education laws were repealed in 1782.

HEDGE SCHOOLMASTERS

The hedge schoolmasters of the nineteenth century were the last repositories of a high tradition.

Patrick Pearse, *The Murder Machine*

The schoolmasters were the cast-off heirs of the '*filí*' or poet-scholars who had enjoyed patronage under Gaelic elites but found themselves without a role after the collapse of the Gaelic order in the early seventeenth century. This led to a class of itinerant scholars wandering the countryside, making use of their learning by teaching for a living. It was no doubt because of the calibre of learning amongst the masters that the hedge schools gained a reputation for imparting elite subjects like Latin and Greek.

Apprentice teachers, or 'poor scholars', trained under schoolmasters until such time as they felt ready to put themselves forward for what must be one of the most stress-inducing exam processes ever conceived. This was 'The Challenge': a public battle of wits and learning between a master and his apprentice presided over by the local parish priest. An unsuccessful challenge would result in a return to the apprenticeship. If the candidate was successful they were free to seek further instruction under another master or to open their own school.

Hedge schoolmasters were an entrepreneurial sort. They would advertise their schools with a public notice, perhaps on the door of the church or in a local newspaper. It was a highly competitive profession: there was an average of six schools per rural parish. The ads were presented in attractive copperplate handwriting with a list of the subjects available. There was a very high demand for reading and writing in the English language. But subject lists were quite varied. Latin, for instance, was in demand for those bound for the priesthood. There was also some demand for arithmetic, navigation, bookkeeping and Greek. The cost for instruction in reading was 1 shilling and Latin 11 shillings. Schoolmasters would often accept payment in kind of butter, eggs or turf. Payment was inconsistent and ultimately it was a peripatetic existence: one teacher taught in sixteen locations over twelve years.

There were also schoolmistresses. They did not live as poor scholars, and would generally stop teaching once they married. They would often have worked with schoolmasters, or they may have learned from a parent who taught or married a master. Male masters too would often marry if they were able to settle in an area (more likely after the repeal of the penal laws in 1782).

SCHOOL DAY

Pupils generally receive only a few years of education, maybe between the ages of five and ten, though there were some schools with pupils in their late teens and early twenties. In general, they received only the 'Three Rs' and some religion.

As children also worked on the family farm, their attendance was by no means regular, being dependent on the season. Long journeys to school on foot meant that the weather was also a factor in attendance.

On average schools would have contained about forty-three pupils, though some had up to 100. It must have been difficult for one master to teach these kinds of numbers and range of ages, and there is some evidence that a 'monitorial' system was used i.e. older pupils might have taken charge of some younger groups. The result was what one historian called 'enlightened chaos'. It was common practice to have several lessons proceeding at once, with different groups busy with different activities. In most schools the day seems to have been broken into alternate periods of lesson-learning and examination by the master, thereby keeping several groups busy. Reading aloud was a common method of teaching reading, which must have produced an awful cacophony as pupils would have been reading from different books. Oral repetition featured, though this was often a form of showmanship for passers-by and visitors. Play was also allowed while the master was with another group.

SCHOOLBOOKS

There were no set textbooks and one Commission of Inquiry found reading materials as diverse as the Mutiny Act, the New Testament and *The Pleasant Art of Money Catching*. Commissioners also found *Fair Rosamund, Mistress to Henry II*, *History of Donna Rosina (a Spanish courtesan)*, *History of Irish Rogues and Rapparees* and *History of Freney, a notorious robber*. Even more worryingly there were copies of Rousseau and Voltaire. Needless to say much of this reading material was a cause of concern for the authorities as was the idea that schoolmasters were spreading radical and seditious notions about revolution around the countryside. One begins to understand why they wanted to bring the education system under control.

NATIONAL SCHOOLS

The Irish National School System was set up in 1831; the first centralised, State-run system in the United Kingdom.

The national schools were certainly a success in terms of numbers. In 1834, out of an estimated population requiring education of 570,000 they were already providing education for 107,000 and by 1852, even after the terrible decimation of the Famine, the number had increased to 544,000.

Neutrality

The national school system founded on the principle of religious neutrality: schools were to be non-denominational and Catholic and Protestant children were to be educated together. Four days a week were to be spent on general instruction, with a further day for denominational religious instruction under the superintendence of the relevant local clergy.

There were quite a number of complaints made to the commissioners regarding violations of their rules on religious and political neutrality. Complaints were made about political meetings taking place in schoolrooms and the use of schoolrooms for public worship. In 1834, it was claimed that an anti-Union meeting had taken place at Loughrea National School (the commissioners disagreed) while Casltercomer female school was struck off the national school list on the grounds that its schoolroom had sometimes been used as part of the chapel adjoining it.

Individual teachers were accused of attending political meetings, and of being members of political clubs and organisations. Mr McIvor, a teacher in Ballymun National School, County Wexford, was accused of selling swords and pikes in the year of rebellion, 1848 (he was, naturally enough, dismissed). Some very scrupulous policing of religious and political neutrality went on: Revd Doherty of Omagh complained in 1851 that one of the local schoolteachers had 'orange flowers in the window of his kitchen' (the commissioners replied that they were 'anxious at all times to discourage, and prevent any exhibition of party feeling' but that Revd Doherty had failed to supply any particulars of the case).

In reality, the schools were only non-denominational in name. By 1870 half of Catholic children were attending schools without any Protestants, while a further 45 per cent were attending schools in which only one out of fifteen were Protestant. Alexis de Tocqueville, a French traveller, visited Carlow in 1835 and remarked that the national school for girls was conducted in a convent and by nuns. The Catholic priests, he noted, 'appeared extremely pleased with these schools, a further proof that they are entirely used by the Catholic party'. Perhaps this explains why, on the whole, the Catholic clergy accepted the new system.

The Protestant clergy, by contrast, were vehemently opposed. They were especially exercised that the education system did not have the use of the full Scripture at its heart and core. Tensions on the issue of the national schools ran very high. *The Warder*, an evangelical newspaper, wrote 'We shall rejoice to see this Jesuitical scheme for the gradual extinction of Protestantism in Ireland defeated ... we adjure Protestant and Presbyterian – all Christians of the Reformation, not to subscribe one shilling to any school under the government of the Board'.

Schoolbooks

As part of their effort to ensure religious impartiality the Board of National School Commissioners published their own schoolbooks for use in the classroom. Many have complained that these demonstrated a clear anti-Irish bias, or at least a clear pro-English and pro-Empire bias.

Most famously, the the following lines from a hymn by Jane Taylor were to be hung in classrooms:

I thank the goodness and the grace
Which on my birth have smiled,
And made me in these Christian days,
A happy English child.

Certainly, there were unionist connotations behind the following appeal to religious toleration:

The people of these islands have one and the same language (all at least who are educated), one and the same Queen – the same laws; and though they differ in their religious worship, they all serve the same God, and call themselves by the name of Christ. All of this is enough to make them brethern, in spite of many disagreements and faults which history tells of them in their intercourse with each other ... a better knowledge of duty will give future history better things to record.

In a lesson on modern history it was noted that in recent years Catholic Emancipation had been granted, 'and the Union between Britain and Ireland has been completed. These measures afford great promise of imparting new vigour to the empire, and of raising that portion of it, which is at present in a state of depression, to its just level'. In a geography book, the children were given the following warning: 'The people of Ireland are a clever, lively people; formerly, very much given to drink, and very ignorant; but now it is believed that they are one of the soberest nations of Europe; and it will be their own fault if they are not also one of the best educated'.

EDUCATION IN THE FREE STATE

The concern of governments after independence was to reverse the anglicising effects of the national schools. They took to this task with some gusto, ensuring that the primary school curriculum was dominated by the Irish language and the Catholic religion.

The government perservered with their language policy despite the opposition of teachers. One teacher from Achill, County Mayo, tried to explain the problem to the government:

If it could be brought home to the parents that their children stand to gain something by their speaking Irish ... you might have a remedy. As it is they are opposed to Irish. They see people with English getting all the jobs ... It is just a question of bread and butter. You cannot blame them because everything practically is denied to them if they don't know English.

A priest from Killarney noted 'If you urge Irish speaking the reply is: "What good is Irish in America?".' The government did not agree. Éamon de Valera, the Minister for Education in 1940, noted that 'I cannot see that parents, as a body, can decide in this matter'. The policy was pursued regardless of any parental criticism.

The government likewise ignored the pleas of teachers who argued that the emphasis on Irish was taking time from other subjects. They also argued tendency of the government's language policy in schools, which emphasised written over spoken Irish, 'is towards making Irish almost a dead language'. The State's efforts to revive the language as the *lingua franca* via the school system failed.

The whole tenor of the curriculum was nationalistic. The teaching of history was to 'develop the best traits of the national character and to inculcate national pride and self-respect. This will not be attained by the cramming of dates and details but rather by showing that the Irish race has fulfilled a great mission in the advancement of civilization and that, on the whole, the Irish nation has amply justified its existence'.

The place of the Catholic religion and the influence of the Catholic Church in education was another striking feature. A clear statement of the Catholic Church's view on denominationalism was presented in a statement by the Catholic Primary Managers' Association in 1922: 'we wish to assert the great fundamental principle that the only satisfactory system of education for Catholics is one wherein Catholic children are taught in Catholic schools by Catholic teachers under Catholic control'.

According to the Church, the role of the State was subordinate to theirs in matters of education. The State at the time agreed that the Church should have the dominant role.

The Church was opposed to co-educational schools, with the bishops noting in 1926: 'mixed education in public schools is very undesirable, especially among older children'. In 1934 the Church issued an episcopal ban on any lay involvement in the management of national schools. Although much of this power has been eroded in practical terms, it is still the case that 96 per cent of Irish schools are under denominational patronage.

FREE SECONDARY EDUCATION

In Northern Ireland, the 1947 Education Act provided for universal free secondary education. It was another twenty years before fees were abolished in the Republic of Ireland.

In 1960 a Council of Education report had declared free secondary education to be 'untenable and utopian'. Nonetheless, six years later the Minister for Education, Donagh O'Malley, announced that from September 1967, secondary education was to be made free. His announcement, made at a seminar organised by the National Union of Journalists, came as a surprise to both the Minister for Finance and the rest of the Cabinet. Nonetheless, it effected a revolution in Irish education.

7

LAW

EARLY IRISH LAW

Brehon Law

Brehon Law is the name given to the early Irish system of law. It developed from legal customs that were passed down orally from generation to generation. These were set down in writing in the seventh century for the first time. The laws were administered by Brehons, the successors of the Celtic druids, and they preserved and interpreted the law, acting as arbitrators rather than judges. The Anglo-Normans brought with them English common law but Brehon law survived up until the early seventeenth century in areas outside English control.

Marriage

Bretha Crolige is an early Irish legal document which refers to the three lawful wives that a man may have (with reference to the Old Testament to bolster the argument): the principal wife, the concubine and the mistress. Polygamy was practiced by the upper classes at this time, and divorce and remarriage was a feature of life. Brian Boru, for instance, in an effort to prevent war, formed some strategic alliances by marrying both the mother of the Hiberno-Norse King of Dublin and the sister of the King of Leinster.

The grounds for divorce were either remarkably honest or remarkably horrible, depending on your point of view. A man had grounds for divorce if his wife was unfaithful, attempted an abortion, was a thief, brought shame on her husband's honour, smothered her child or was 'without milk through sickness'. Meanwhile, a woman had grounds for divorce if her husband was unfaithful, failed to provide support, spread false stories about her, was impotent, obese, homosexual, sterile, very indiscreet about the marriage or in holy orders. While the Church condemned divorce, it continued to be availed of, at least amongst the Gaelic aristocracy, until the seventeenth century.

Under the Gaelic custom, women's relations with their families remained intact after marriage, which gave them a degree of independence. It also seems that women could petition for divorce as easily as men, and if the divorce was accepted on her petition she could retain any wealth she had brought to the marriage. In a divorce settlement the woman would also receive a share of the profits generated while in the union.

The wealthy undertook trial marriages, meaning that cohabitation was probably allowed. The legal age for marriage for girls was fifteen and for boys it was eighteen.

The Anglo-Normans brought a different set of marriage customs in the twelfth century, reflecting English common law and canon law. In this tradition, the bride's family relinquished her completely and she became her husband's responsibility. All of her property was transferred to her husband's estate. In Gaelic society, concubines were accorded the same status as wives and their children were not deprived of in inheritance rights, whereas under common law only legitimate children inherited. Ultimately, the extension of English common law began to influence marriage customs. A growing concern with inheritance and legitimacy made legally contracted marriages preferable.

Prior to the Norman invasion it was common for priests and monks to marry, and even after the invasion little changed. The authorities classed these women as concubines, though they seem to have been treated the same as wives were.

Honour

Early Irish legal practitioners demonstrated a flair for metaphors. '*Enech*' or 'face' was used in various ways to denote 'honour'. For instance, an insult and the payment needed to compensate for it is '*enechruicce*', 'face-reddening', while compensation for outraged honour is also referred to as '*enechlann*', 'face-cleaning'. In one legal text, it is noted that there were three things that could wash the dirt of offences from the face: the 'pumice stone' of publicly admitting a fault; the 'water' of payment for damages; and the 'towel' of penance according to a penitential.

A free man's status is expressed as '*lóg n-enech*', 'The value of the face'. This was an actual quantitative value that could be calculated – an 'honour price' – that rose according to rank. This value was used as the basis of compensation payments. The unit of value was the '*cumal*' or 'female slave', though prices were usually paid in cattle, gold or silver (one cumal = three milch cows). A king was worth seven cumal.

The rules for compensation appear to have been important. With regard to theft, compensation had to be made to two people: the owner of the thing stolen and the owner of the land or building from which the thing was stolen. This might of course be the same person, in which case that person is compensated with two payments. The payment to the owner of the land on which the thing was stolen was calculated according to where the theft took place. Thus, if something was stolen from inside a house full *lóg n-enech* of the victim was paid; if it was stolen from outside the proportion of the *lóg n-enech* to be paid depended on the distance from the house.

Bee Judgments

Beekeeping and honey making were important in Ireland, possibly because without sugar it was the only sweetening agent available. Honey was also used to make mead and beeswax to make candles. So, all in all, bees were a resource. There was a detailed legal tract relating to bees, honey and hives: 'Bechbretha', Bee Judgments. These included a law for compensation if one was stung by another man's bees; the owner was responsible for the crimes of his bees. Since bees owned by an individual obtain nectar from the area surrounding their hive, the four farms adjacent to the hive were entitled to a small proportion of the honey produced and after the third year they were entitled to a swarm.

Law of the Innocents

The Church could also contribute to the law. The abbot of Iona, Adomnán, initiated a set of laws known as the Law of the Innocents that were enacted in Birr in 697. The Law of the Innocents was concerned with protecting non-combatants in war and other vulnerable people. It stopped women taking part in warfare, for instance. It also stated that if a woman was slain, the killer was to have his right hand and left foot cut off before death. The law further outlined sanctions against the killing of children, clerics, clerical students and peasants on clerical lands. It detailed compensation for various crimes against women:

> If it be forcible rape of a girl, half of seven cumals for it. If it be a hand [touching] against her or on her belt, ten ounces for it ... If it be [putting] a hand under her clothing to dishonour her, one cumal and three ounces for it ... If a woman has been made pregnant through fornication, without contract, without property, without bride-price, without betrothal, full fines for it.

COPYRIGHT

In 561 St Columba borrowed a psalter from St Finian, and made a copy of it. Finian demanded that both the book and its copy be handed to him, but Columba refused. The matter was taken to the High King Diarmuid at Tara. Diarmuid ruled in favour of Finian stating: '*Le gach bain a bainin, le gach leabhar a leabhrán*', 'To every cow its calf, to every book, its copy'. This is the first recorded ruling on copyright.

Columba refused to accept the ruling, however, and the subsequent Battle of Cul Dremhne in 561 saw 3,000 dead. Columba's men won the battle, but afterwards, stricken with guilt, he left Ireland for Iona where he founded his famous monastery.

STATUES OF KILKENNY

The Statutes of Kilkenny were passed in 1367 and were a response by the English lordship to the threat of the resurgent Gaelic Irish and to the erosion of English power because of an apparent dilution of Englishness. Quite simply, the English were becoming too Irish. As the statutes note:

> Now many English of the said land, forsaking the English language, manners, mode of riding, laws and usages, live and govern themselves according to the manners, fashion, and language of the Irish enemies; and also have made divers marriages and alliances between themselves and the Irish enemies aforesaid; whereby the said land, and the liege people thereof, the English language, the allegiance due to our lord the king, and the English laws there, are put in subjection and decayed, and the Irish enemies exalted and raised up.

The aim was thus to 'decontaminate' the colony and enable it to defend itself.

The rules forbade any kind of alliance between English and Irish by marriage, by standing as godparents, by fostering of children or by concubinage. Every English person was to use the English language, the English version of their names and 'The English custom, fashion, mode of riding and apparel, according to his estate'. Any man with land or rent more than £100 per year must ride with a saddle in the English fashion. If he was found contravening this, his horse would be forfeited, and he would be thrown in prison and fined. Clergy living in the English colony were given until the Feast of St Michael to learn English and get saddles. They were to use English thereafter. The native Irish were no longer be given ecclesiastical benefices or admitted to religious houses in the lordship. No Irish entertainers 'pipers, story-tellers, bablers, rimers, mowers, nor any other Irish agent' were to be allowed amongst the English or given any patronage lest they act as spies. Brehon law was dismissed as a 'bad custom' and common law was to govern the English.

The statutes wanted to obliterate any distinctions between the English in England and the English in Ireland, noting that no difference of allegiance was henceforth to be made 'by calling them English hobbe, or Irish dog'. They were all to be called 'The English lieges of our Lord the King'.

There were various other clauses concerned with preparations for war. For example, Englishmen were not to sell any horses or armour to an Irishman, or victuals in a time of war. The legislation did not have a lasting effect but it was also not repealed until the parliament of 1613–15

PENAL LAWS

The laws began in the 1690s as a series of discriminatory measures introduced by the Irish parliament which were eventually dismantled in 1778, 1782 and 1792–93. The laws reflected the hardening of Irish Protestant attitudes following experiences under Catholic James II. The Williamite wars (1689–91) had seen the defeat of the Jacobites but Protestants still felt like a vulnerable minority. In particular, after the Treaty of Limerick in 1691, largely left the Catholic landed interest intact. Therefore, the harshest penal laws were instituted against Catholic property. Property was, apparently, power.

As part of the law, Catholics were forbidden to carry weapons, to go overseas for education and to teach or run schools. Clergy and bishops were banned, except secular priests who were allowed to remain, albeit limited to one per parish. No clergy were allowed to enter the kingdom. The most significant legislation was the Act to Prevent the Further Growth of Popery (1704), which prohibited Catholics buying land, inheriting land from Protestants or taking leases from longer than thirty-one years. Estates of deceased Catholic landowners were to be divided equally among male heirs. Catholics were also prohibited from practising law, holding office in central or local government and from service in the navy or army. They were excluded from parliament but did not completely lose right to vote until 1728.

Scholarship has shown that the Penal Laws were selective in their operation. The Catholic aristocracy were the main targets, being deprived of the opportunity to extend estates and engage in politics, and many converted to Church of Ireland. The ban on bishops and clergy entering the kingdom should have resulted in the death of the clergy, but there was no sustained attempt to enforce this law or to promote a mass conversion to Protestantism. By the 1720s, priests and bishops operated freely, if discreetly, in most areas. According to a 1731 report on the state of Popery almost every diocese had a bishop. Clerical numbers rose and ass houses continued to be built.

The laws were repealed by the English parliament after the end of the war with France, when there was less threat of an allegiance between Ireland and France. They were also trying to discourage Catholics finding cause with the Volunteers, an armed politically active force set up in 1778 to defend country and champion Catholic relief.

TREASON

United Irishmen

The first United Irish leaders to be tried, found guilty, and executed for high treason were brothers John and Henry Sheares. They were hanged together outside Newgate Prison in Dublin in front of a large crowd. Their bodies were cut down and beheaded.

One man executed as member of the United Irishmen was the victim of a terrible miscarriage of justice. Sir Edward William Crosbie was a well-born barrister. Of liberal views and popular, he was a member of the lawyer's corps of the Irish Volunteers. After practising at the bar for seven years, he took up residence outside Carlow town. At 2 o'clock on the morning of 25 May 1798 a band of 1,200 rebels assembled on his lawn and demanded that he lead them. He refused to accompany, aid or abet them: he was never a member of the United Irishmen. The rebels proceeded to attack Carlow but were defeated, the garrison having been forewarned. Many were arrested and summarily executed. Sometime around 30 May, Crosbie was arrested and on 2, 4 and 5 June was tried by court-martial for aiding and abetting rebels. Despite flimsy evidence and efforts by himself, his wife and friends, he was found guilty and hanged on 5 June; his head placed on a pike and displayed above Carlow Jail with three others. According to Valentine Lawless he was 'executed by torch light a few hours before the arrival of an order from the lord lieutenant for his transmission to Dublin'.

Emmet and Tone

Robert Emmet was arrested after the rebellion he organised in 1803. Emmet had instructed his lawyers not to make any defence and when convicted of treason he delivered a long and eloquent speech from the dock defending his rebellion and creating his legacy while he still lived. He was hanged outside St Catherine's church on Thomas Street. After thirty minutes his limp corpse was taken down and his head cut from his body; the executioner holding it up to cry: 'This is the head of a traitor, Robert Emmet. This is the head of a traitor'.

Emmet's rebellion was, in a sense, a delayed second act to the 1798 rebellion led by Theobald Wolfe Tone. Wolfe Tone's trial, like Emmet's, resulted in a sentence of death. He had been captured stepping off a French ship, coming ashore after perhaps the greatest sea battle fought in Irish waters. He was brought in chains to Dublin to face a military court in the Royal Barracks. Like Emmet, he did not fight the charges. His request to be shot by firing squad was denied: he was to be hanged as a traitor. He tried to cut his throat instead. The authorities, grimly determined to hang their traitor, sewed up his windpipe but he died a week later from the wounds.

1916 Leaders

More recent history delivered to Ireland her most famous martyrs. The leaders of the 1916 Rising were found guilty of treason and executed. Patrick Pearse, Thomas J. Clarke, Thomas MacDonagh, Joseph Mary Plunkett, Edward (Ned) Daly, William Pearse, Michael O'Hanrahan, John MacBride, Éamonn Ceannt, Michael Mallin, Cornelius Colbert, Seán Heuston, Seán MacDiarmada, James Connolly and Thomas Kent: all were shot by firing squad in May 1916.

Another participant in the events leading up to the Rising was put to death: Roger Casement. Casement had visited Germany to obtain arms for the rebels in 1914, but feeling the amount of arms promised by the Germans was inadequate, he made his way back to Ireland in 1916 to postpone the planned rising and was arrested after landing. His trial for treason was a media sensation. There were many appeals on his behalf. To discredit him, the government circulated extracts of his diaries detailing homosexual activity. He was hanged in England in August 1916, the last 1916 martyr. His remains were returned to Ireland in 1965 where he received a State funeral.

Lord Haw Haw

William Joyce, also known as 'Lord Haw Haw', was found guilty of treason for broadcasting Nazi propaganda to Britain during the war. Born in Brooklyn, New York, in 1906, Joyce grew up in Mayo and Galway. A fervent imperialist who consorted with, and acted as a scout for, the Black and Tans during the War of Independence, one contemporary recalled that his views were so extreme that even loyalists disliked him. Fleeing to England in 1921 to join the army, he became a fascist, eventually working for Oswald Mosley's British Union of Fascists (he was sacked in 1937).

His admiration for Nazi Germany saw him leave Britain for Berlin in 1939. He began working for an English-language radio service at the State broadcasting company, finding an outlet for his forceful rhetorical style. Goebbels was a fan. His broadcasts gained a wide audience in Britain, where people were fascinated by a chance to hear the enemy in their homes. Initially a figure of fun, he became widely despised, although some in Ireland enjoyed his anti-British taunts. He made a final, defiant broadcast on the day of Hitler's death before attempting to flee to Sweden. He was captured in May 1945, brought back to Britain, and tried. At his trial he pointed to the fact that he was born in America, but because he had falsely acquired a British passport in 1933 (claiming to have been born in Ireland) he was said to have incurred duties of allegiance. He was hanged in January 1946. He was reinterred in Ireland in 1976 due to fears his grave would become a fascist shrine in England.

EXECUTIONS

'Lady Betty'

One executioner was recruited from amongst the soon-to-be-executed. 'Lady Betty' was a feared hangwoman at Roscommon Jail. Though it is difficult to separate fact from fiction, the story is sad, grisly and terrifying. Betty and her only surviving son were left destitute after her husband's death and their eviction. Probably from County Kerry, they made their way to Roscommon, where they squatted in a derelict cottage and begged. After a time her son left for America, and though he wrote, Betty was left increasingly embittered and lonely. Years later a finely dressed man called to her home looking for shelter. In the still watches of the night, Betty drove a knife through the stranger, so she could rob him. Rifling through his possessions, she realised it was her son who had returned from America with his new-found wealth. She gave herself up and was sentenced to be hanged. When the official executioner took ill, Betty volunteered to perform that day's executions in return for her life. So good was she that it became her occupation. She was made the official executioner with a wage and lodgings in the jail. She had a habit of drawing sketches of her swinging victims and also performed public floggings, apparently with enthusiasm. The 1798 rebellion kept her busy and the Lord Lieutenant officially lifted her sentence in 1802 in recognition of her contribution to making Roscommon a safer place. She died in 1807.

The Haughton Drop

Samuel Haughton (1821–97), geologist, physiologist and mathematician, was responsible for a humane advancement in hanging. In earlier centuries, hanging was not meant to instantly kill the victim, but was a prelude to drawing and quartering. Civilisation had outgrown those latter two tortures, and hanging was made the mode of execution. Haughton felt it was also time to render this aspect less horrendous. He invented the 'Haughton Drop' which was calculated to ensure that the drop would be long enough to kill the victim instantly, rather than leave them dangling in strangling agony. In case you were wondering, a person weighing 140lbs would need to drop 15ft. The Haughton Drop was eventually adopted across Europe.

DUELLING

The Irish were enthusiastic and proficient duellers. Prior to 1800, there were nineteen companies making or selling duelling pistols in Dublin alone. Research has shown that the death rate from duelling in Ireland was estimated to be one in four, compared with England where it was one in fourteen.

Daniel O'Connell once killed a man in a duel. O'Connell refused to apologise for his criticism of Dublin Corporation's treatment of Catholics and was challenged to a duel by a member of the Corporation, John D'Esterre. The duel took place on 2 February 1815 at Bishopscourt, near Naas, County Kildare. Both men fired at the same time. D'Esterre missed but O'Connell wounded D'Esterre, who died the following day. O'Connell came to regret his actions and it burned his conscience for the rest of his life. He vowed never to fight again. Duelling went into decline around this period.

The only surviving code of conduct for duelling in the world is one that was adopted in Clonmel in 1777.

Between 1771 and 1790, the most common reason for duelling was insults, followed by politics and elections and, in third place, women.

REVISING THE LAW

In 2012, Minister Brian Hayes introduced the Statute Law Revision Bill to repeal almost 22,000 laws. According to the minister, this was not only the largest mass repealing measure in the history of the State, but the largest 'single statute law revisions measure' in any jurisdiction. There had been several previous Statute Law Revision Acts that examined pre-1922 legislation to see what pre-independence legislation could be discarded with which might usefully be retained.

8

RELIGION

ST PATRICK

My name is Patrick. I am a sinner, a simple country person, and the least of all believers.

So begins the *Confessio* of St Patrick. Many people might be surprised to learn that this fifth-century missionary to Ireland left some writings. In fact, he left both his *Confessio* and *Epistola*. Locating the real, historical Patrick has proved difficult, however. He notes that he was taken prisoner near Bannavem Taburniae at about sixteen but even locating Bannavem Taburniae has proved impossible. It is thought that it was somewhere on the west coast of Britain. Patrick was born in Roman Britain to a clerical family of moderate means (his father was a deacon). He returned to Britain after six years of slavery in Ireland, but later came back as a missionary. It is interesting, if somewhat disappointing, to note what is not mentioned in the *Confessio*: there are no shamrocks, no snakes, no mountains where he tended sheep (no Slieve Mis or Croagh Patrick), no fire on the Hill of Tara. All of these were added to the narrative with time.

IRISH CHRISTIANITY

It could be said that Irish Catholicism has often seemed like paganism bursting out of ill-fitting Christian clothes. Even well into the twentieth century there were parts of the country where Catholic domestication had not quite tamed the pagan spirit.

Superstitions

Travellers to Ireland often remarked on the deeply superstitious nature of the people. The subtext was, of course, a contrast with the rational Christianity of their readers.

William Lithgow in his account of his travels in 1619 described the Irish as 'only titular Christians'. Their ignorance seemed almost to offend him. He claimed that hundreds 'of better than the common sort' asked him if Jerusalem was in Ireland and St Patrick's purgatory was the Holy Land. They seemed to endow the moon with supernatural powers:

> At the fight of each new moon, (I speak it credibly), bequeath their cattle to her protection, humbly imploring the pale lady of the night, that she will leave their bestial in as good plight as she found them; and if sick, scabbed, or sore, they solicit her maiden-faced Majesty to restore them to their health.

Fynes Moryson, who lived in Ireland at the start of the seventeenth century, took note of some superstitions such as: believing somebody will die if a black spot is found on a mutton bone; that ill-luck will befall horses if the rider, having eaten eggs, does not wash his hands or pick equally sized eggs; that falling on the ground requires turning around three times towards the right-hand side and digging up a sod of earth with a knife or sword to prevent bad luck. The Irish were also offended if somebody commended their cattle unless they said 'God save them' or, alternatively, spit on them.

Patterns

The Christianising of pre-existing pagan festivals and feasts is not unique to Ireland. And like many rural countries, the old beliefs often proved stubborn. Patterns were local religious festivals held at holy wells or other places on the feast day of the saint to whom the site is dedicated. Pattern is derived from the Irish '*patrún*' meaning patron.

By the eighteenth century patterns were venues for popular sociability, typically combining a procession to the site with prayers and other observances on arrival, with dancing, drinking and other festive capering. Given this mixture of raucous sociability and pious solemnity it is thought that patterns may have originally been pagan festivities which were overlaid with some Christian seriousness.

The Catholic clergy went on the rampage against patterns in the nineteenth century as they sought to bring the Church under control, impose greater uniformity of practice and cattle-drive public morals into the pen. The Famine, along with the spread of education and affluence to rural areas, meant that by the 1870s most patterns had disappeared from the festive calendar.

Pope

Ireland can lay claim to a pope. Or a pope-elect, at least. St Benedict was born in Durrow in present-day County Laois. He became a follower of St Enda and in 522 accompanied him to Rome. While they were still there the following year the pope died and the elders of the Church met to elect a successor. Benedict had by all accounts acquired a reputation for prayer and sanctity which so impressed them that he was elected pope. He initially accepted (he apparently chose the name Pupeus). Enda was about to set off to return home to Galway, when Benedict reconsidered; whether because of homesickness or cold feet is unclear. He retired to pray and on emerging declined the papacy. John Paul I was elected instead and Enda and Benedict returned home. The Irishman was pope-elect for two days.

JEWISH COMMUNITY

There was probably a Jewish community in Ireland as early as 1232, as a grant in July of that year makes reference to Jewish inhabitants. By the eighteenth century there was an established community in Dublin comprising about 200 persons. Daniel O'Connell, who fought for Catholic civil rights, was also responsible for the repeal of an obsolete British law, 'De Judaismo', which prescribed particular dress for Jews. He noted: 'Ireland has claims on your ancient race; it is the only country that I know of unsullied by one act of persecution of the Jews'.

By 1901 the population had risen to an estimated 3,771, as people arrived from Eastern Europe (particularly Lithuania) in the wake of Russian pogroms. By 1904 it was closer to 4,800, mainly in Dublin. That same year of 1904 witnessed what became known as the Limerick pogrom, led by a Redemptorist priest who was afterwards sent to an island in the Pacific. The result of this campaign of anti-Semitic sermons, newspaper articles and boycotting businesses meant that almost all Jews in Limerick fled the city. John Redmond and Michael Davitt both condemned the campaign.

Ireland did not provide much of a refuge for Jews fleeing Nazi persecution: it is estimated that only about thirty Jews were admitted as refugees before and during the Second World War. Nonetheless, the Jewish population rose to about 5,500 in the 1940s. The areas around Lower Clanbrassil Street and the South Circular Road in Dublin became known as 'Little Jerusalem' owing to the presence of Jewish residences and businesses and in the 1902 Dublin Corporation elections James Connolly distributed his leaflets in the area in Yiddish. The Irish Jewish Museum is located in the vicinity today and houses a Guinness bottle with a label in Hebrew.

Many Jews left after the Second World War (bound for Israel or the United States) and today the population stands at about 1,800.

RELIGIOUS CONTROVERSIES

It is hard for us to get our secular heads around the fact in the eighteenth and nineteenth centuries issues of religious doctrine could generate bitter controversy. This was the age of pamphlet literature, where interested parties would publish their opinions in the full expectation of receiving a written reply. Thus you might have *A reply to Patrick M'Carrol's pamphlet: entitled, the Catholic faith vindicated. With observations, on the doctrines of purgatory, good works meritorious, transubstantiation, and priests forgiving sins* (1824), which you can be fairly sure disagreed with Patrick views. People even suggested future topics for debate in the title of a pamphlet: *Reply to the Rev. Dr. H. Cooke including, at his request, a critique on his report of 'The Belfast discussion', and an offer to discuss with him 'The Question of questions'* (1836).

Expressing controversial views could have serious consequences. In 1702, a Unitarian minister in Dublin, Thomas Emlyn was fined £1,000 and imprisoned for one year for publishing a pamphlet in which he rejected the doctrine of the Trinity and the divinity of Christ, while in 1794, a Trinity College student called John Burk was expelled for expressing his heretical anti-Trinitarian beliefs.

Controversies often arose when the Catholic Church was offered any apparent support from the State. In 1795, St Patrick's College, Maynooth was established as a seminary for the training of Catholic priests by An Act for the Better Education of Persons Professing the Popish or Roman Catholic Religion. Prior to this priests had trained on the Continent, but the French Revolution had closed many of these educational establishments. The government was attempting to court Catholic support and Maynooth College was a gesture of conciliation. In 1845, the Prime Minister Robert Peel proposed that the grant be increased. This was met with howls of protest. One petition stated that the grant represented no less than 'a violation of the constitutional charter of the realm – an infringement of God's most holy law, which denounces idolatry and superstition, and as a direct encouragement to the continuance of that disloyalty and disaffection which has so long disgraced our unhappy land'. Even Queen Victoria expressed her alarm at this vitriol, writing, 'I am sure poor Peel ought to be *blessed* by all Catholics for the many and noble ways in which he stands forth to protect and do good for poor Ireland. But the bigotry, the wicked and blind passion it brings forth is quite dreadful, and I blush for Protestantism!'

Obviously in the mood for controversy, Peel went further and founded the Queen's Colleges in 1845. These were non-denominational universities, designed to give Catholics access to third level education, since at the time Trinity College Dublin, Ireland's only university was a Protestant institution. The Queen's Colleges were established in Belfast, Cork and Galway. Like the earlier founding of Maynooth, these too were designed to conciliate Catholics and undermine the Repeal of the Union movement. The more militant Catholic bishops and clergy were vehemently opposed. Even O'Connell, denounced the 'godless colleges'.

Catholic rejection of the Queen's Colleges led to the establishment of the Catholic University founded by the Irish bishops in 1853. The founding rector was John Henry Newman. While it struggled initially (Newman resigned after five years) in 1882 it became University College, Dublin. Meanwhile, the Queen's Colleges survive today as Queen's Belfast, NUIG and UCC.

RELIGIOUS DIVISIONS

Swaddler

'Swaddler' was a term of abuse for evangelicals. It came from 'Swaddling John' Cennick, a Moravian who was the first to bring the 'Great Awakening' to Ireland in 1746, a year before the arrival of John Wesley, the founder of Methodism. Cennick proved a popular preacher. When a reference to the Babe 'in swaddling clothes' was misunderstood by his audience, he was given the name 'Swaddling John'. The name grew feet: Wesley found himself being called 'swaddler' by children in the street when he arrived and it eventually became a derogatory term for an evangelical.

There is an irony here in that Cennick was as inoffensive as he could possibly be. He deliberately avoided arousing passionate denominational feelings, was not doctrinally dogmatic and was not interested in proselytising amongst Catholics (though he welcomed them to his meetings) but in reviving the enthusiasm of the 'saved'.

He went on to found ten chapels and over 200 religious societies in Ulster, mainly around Lough Neagh. He died prematurely at the age of thirty-six, most of his last ten years having been spent in Ireland, worn down physically and mentally by his great efforts.

The Second Reformation

The 1820s and 1830s was the age of the 'Second Reformation'. Evangelical Protestants of an active and missionary bent began the last great effort to convert the Irish Catholic population *en masse*, and bring about a Second Reformation where the first had clearly failed. Numerous evangelical societies took part in this effort, and at times it appeared they were engaged in competitive efforts to invent the most cumbersome name. There was the Society for Irish Church Missions; the Irish Society for Promoting the Education of the Native Irish through Medium of their own Language; and the Association for Discountenancing Vice and Promoting Religion and Virtue.

The Churches battled for the consciences of the people and while there were many well-meaning people, some of the tactics were less than noble. Many Protestant missionaries were accused of 'souperism'. This referred to the use of food relief as a means of converting and proselytising the poor. Essentially, this was a form of bribery bringing new meaning to the words 'food for the soul'. It is often associated with the Great Famine, but also applied to earlier missionary efforts. Some Protestant missionaries described similar tactics being used by Catholics to win back converts to their original religion, for example offers of land or schools being set up providing food and clothes.

Elizabeth Jane Whately, an active Protestant evangelical, wrote a history of the Luke Street Girls Home where she volunteered, recounting that many who arrived at the school, 'came as bigoted and determined Romanists, resolved not to listen to a word of the Bible teaching they might hear'. She went on to describe one young girl who would chew paper to stuff in her ears during Bible class, until a lesson on purgatory aroused her curiosity enough for her to unblock her ears. They remained unblocked

for every Bible class thereafter. In time she 'declared her faith in Christ as she read of Him in His Word, as her alone Saviour and Mediator'.

The proselytising missions of these enthusiastic clergy and laypeople took them to the remotest parts of Ireland. A missionary 'colony' was set up on the island of Achill in 1834 by the Revd Edward Nangle. It included cottages, schools, an orphanage, a small hospital and a hotel. The local Catholic clergy and laity did not take to the endeavour kindly. In 1836 two men were tried for an assault on a scripture-reader.

In some places where Catholics did convert, they were ostracised, ejected from their homes, denounced from the altar and prevented from earning a living. The Society for Protecting the Rights of Conscience in Ireland was set up in 1850 to save converts to Protestantism from destitution and thereby protect the right to convert. A letter from one missionary in Doon gives a flavour of the mind-set of the Protestant missionaries: 'Many of the converts in Doon rejected the practices and doctrines of the Church of Rome as unreasonable, superstitious, and unscriptural, others were influenced by an anxious intelligent desire for salvation', he wrote. The converts, he wrote, gave evidence of their sincere conversion in many ways, 'especially by regular attendance upon public worship, by sending their children to school, and by neatness and cleanliness in their persons, clothing, and houses; they abstain from drunkenness, faction fights, quarrelling, and illegal combinations, and from idle thriftless habits, to all of which they had been accustomed as Roman Catholics'. As a result of their conversions many had been ejected from their 'hovels' and there were therefore attempts to build 'houses more suitable to the elevated tone of mind of the converts, and more fit for rational beings and Christians'.

It seemed that every awful visitation of famine or sickness provided an arena for religious pugilism. There was an outbreak of cholera in 1832. The deaths of so many seemingly virtuous people had brought forth a rush of evangelical millenarian publication, and a litany of sins that had 'caused' the outbreak were expounded in sermons and pamphlets across Britain. Everything from general offences like drunkenness, blasphemy, pride and arrogance, to more specific circumstances such as divisions within the church and the Reform Bill were cited as reasons why the nation was being called to collective repentance. Others pointed to the condoning of 'Popery' when Catholic Emancipation was granted in 1829 as having brought about the present 'judgment'. These kinds of evangelical providentialist interpretations did not begin to wane until the 1860s. In a country like Ireland, which was riven with sectarian divisions, it was all too easy for one side to blame the other or even blame themselves for giving too much leeway to opponents when awful afflictions appeared.

There was no shortage of evangelical rabble-rousers in Ireland during the nineteenth century. One extreme example was the sectarian message being trumpeted by the millenarian preacher

Tresham Dames Gregg (1800–81). Gregg had been educated at Trinity College, Dublin, and after some time as a curate in the north of England, had returned to Dublin in 1837. He gained a reputation as a militant evangelical, and was made chaplain at Swift's Alley Church in 1840. Gregg drew lots of followers from the Protestant working class and became a folk hero in 1838 after a marathon debate between himself, another evangelical cleric, and two Catholic priests. In 1841, Gregg tried to rescue a young Protestant woman who had reportedly been kidnapped and placed in a nunnery on St George's Hill in Dublin. As it turned out she was a convert to Catholicism, and did not appreciate Gregg's attempts to 'save' her. A crowd gathered outside the convent, and began to pelt Gregg with stones until the constabulary were called and he was placed in the Bridewell Prison for disturbing the peace. On his release a week later, he was greeted by a cheering Protestant mob. The Church of Ireland Archbishop, Richard Whately, was unimpressed with Greggs, describing him as having 'a forty-jackass-power of incessant braying to a mob of low orangemen'. Whately had him banned from preaching in the diocese in 1842, but some supporters took advantage of an ancient prerogative to have him elected him as chaplain of the chantry of St Mary's, which had been free of Episcopal control since the reign of Edward IV. He held the position for the rest of his life, and continued his controversial preaching tours and published attacks on Roman Catholicism until his death in 1881.

9

TRANSPORT, COMMUNICATION AND SCIENCE

TRANSATLANTIC FIRSTS

Telegraph

The first transatlantic telegraph communication was sent from The Telegraph Field, Valencia Island, County Kerry to Newfoundland on 16 August 1858, reducing the time of communication between the continents of Europe and North American from ten day to mere minutes. The communication was a letter of congratulations from Queen Victoria to US President James Buchanan. Unfortunately, the cable only worked for three weeks, but within a decade more durable connections had been established.

Radio Station

In Derrigimlagh Bog, just south of Clifden, County Galway, is the remains of the world's first permanent transatlantic radio station. It was built by radio pioneer Guglielmo Marconi. Marconi had sent a message from Cornwall to Newfoundland, but chose this site in Connemara, where messages could be sent without any land mass to intervene, to establish a huge complex for capacitors, receivers and accommodation for 150 workers. The station opened in 1907 and operated for nine years, sending messages from London and Dublin across the ocean. Eventually, more powerful transmitters were developed meaning stations could move further inland. The station was burnt down during the Troubles and little remains to mark this important site in the history of communications.

Flight

Amazingly, this same bog was the site of another historical transatlantic first. The first non-stop transatlantic flight took off from St Johns, Newfoundland and landed 4 miles south west of Clifden. The flight, undertaken in June 1919 by Jack Alcock and Arthur Whitten Brown, took sixteen hours twenty-seven minutes, travelling at a cruising speed of 90mph and having for long periods to fly no more than 300ft above the surface of the ocean to prevent ice forming. The aircraft was damaged on landing. Spotting the aerials of the Marconi station they came in to land on what looked like a green field from the air but was in fact a bog. The pilots had taken their pet kittens, Twinkletoes and Lucky Jim, with them.

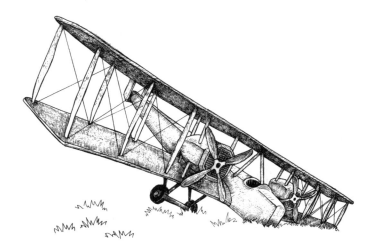

Steamer
The first steamer to cross the Atlantic sailed from Cobh in 1838.

Voyage
Christopher Columbus apparently stopped in Galway before his epic journey across the Atlantic in 1492, saying a prayer in St Nicholas's Cathedral.

SCIENTISTS

Robert Boyle
Robert Boyle (1627–91), in a neat summary of his achievements, is sometimes called the Father of Chemistry. Born in County Waterford, Boyle questioned the validity of alchemy and redefined the remit of chemistry as a science; one that would aim only to determine the composition of substances. His most famous contribution to science, Boyle's Law, states that the pressure and volume of a gas are inversely related at constant temperature. He was one of the founders of the famous Royal Society in London.

William Parsons
William Parsons, third Earl of Rosse (1800–67) is most famous for constructing what was at the time the world's largest telescope in 1845 at Birr Castle, County Offaly. It remained so for seventy years. Parsons could view the heavens in greater detail than anyone else ever had and discovered that many galaxies are spiral shaped.

His son, Charles Parsons (1854–1931), invented the steam turbine in 1884, which revolutionised marine travel and made cheap and plentiful electricity possible.

William Rowan Hamilton
Unquestionably, one of Ireland's greatest scientists, William Rowan Hamilton (1805–65) invented a revolutionary form of algebra in 1843 while walking across the Broom Bridge along Dublin's Royal Canal. A plaque marks the spot: 'Here as he walked by on the 16th of October 1843 Sir William Rowan Hamilton in a flash of genius

discovered the fundamental formula for quaternion multiplication $i^2 = j^2 = k^2 = ijk = -1$ and cut it on a stone of the bridge'.

Hamilton had shown very early promise. By thirteen he had acquired almost as many languages as years, including Persian, Arabic, Hindustani, Sanskrit, and even Marathi and Malay. In September 1813 an American calculating prodigy Zerah Colburn was being exhibited in Dublin. Aged nine to Hamilton's eight, the two were pitted against each other, with Colburn the clear winner. Hamilton resolved to spend less time on languages and more on mathematics.

Quaternions describe things moving in 3D and today are used in computer graphics, control theory, signal processing, and orbital mechanics. He also made important contributions to classical mechanics and optics. For example, Hamilton's principal function helped to establish the wave theory of light. He was also professor of astronomy at Trinity College Dublin and Royal Astronomer of Ireland.

George Boole

George Boole (1815–64) was born in Lincoln, but ended up as the first mathematics professor at Queen's College Cork. His beginnings were modest. His father was a shoemaker and his mother a lady's maid. He was a child prodigy, beginning school at one and a half. At two and a half he went missing and was

found in the centre of Lincoln surrounded by a crowd shouting difficult words for him to spell and was being showered with coins for his correct answers. He taught himself Greek and Latin, and later French, Italian and German. At sixteen he was forced to leave school because of his father's bankruptcy. He became a teacher and opened his own school. He was entirely self-educated in the area of mathematics. In 1841 he founded a new branch of mathematics called Invariant Theory and was awarded the first Gold Medal of the Royal Society for a paper on differential equations.

His main legacy is the invention of a revolutionary way of translating logic into algebraic equations. Boolean algebra would later turn out to be ideal for the manipulation of information in computers.

John Tyndall

John Tyndall (1820–93) was born in County Carlow. He became professor of natural philosophy (i.e. physics) at The Royal Institution and amongst his contributions to science was his pioneering work on radiant heat, germ theory of disease, glacier motion, sound, and diffusion of light in the atmosphere. He explained how gases in the atmosphere trapped heat, warming the earth. He also explained why the sky was blue.

William Thompson

William Thompson (1824–1907), born in Belfast, became professor of natural philosophy at Glasgow University. He introduced the absolute scale of temperature, the Kelvin Scale. His work also led to the second law of thermodynamics.

George Francis FitzGerald

George Francis FitzGerald (1851–1901) was born in Dublin. He was the first to suggest the existence of radio waves and that nothing could travel faster than light. He also postulated that comets were dirty snowballs, composed of snow and gravel.

Ernest Walton

Ernest Walton (1903–97) is Ireland's only Nobel prize-wining scientist. Born in Dungarvan, County Waterford, he was a pioneer of nuclear physics. Together with John Cockroft, he built the first successful particle accelerator at Cambridge with which they split the atom in 1931. He became Professor of Natural and Experimental Philosophy at Trinity College, Dublin in 1946 and in 1951 he and Cockroft were awarded the Nobel Prize.

ELECTRICITY

Rural Electrification

Rural electrification was a fifty-three-year process that was only completed in 2003, when the islands of Inishturbot and Inishturk were connected to the national grid. The rural mainland was completed in 1973. The process began in November 1946, when there were 400,000 farms and rural dwellings in Ireland. By the end of 1959 more than 250,000 rural customers had been connected and by 1965, 80 per cent of rural households could choose to enlighten the gloom. The effects of rural electrification cannot be overstated. Electricity arrived much earlier in urban areas. Dublin had electricity from the 1880s and most towns were electrified by the 1930s.

Ardnacrusha

The Free State government, in what must be acknowledged as an uncharacteristically adventurous move, commissioned the Shannon Hydroelectric scheme, which at the time was the largest hydroelectric station in the world. The scheme was spearheaded by engineer, Thomas McLaughlin, although Robert Kane can be credited with the original idea, having proposed in 1844 that the lower Shannon be harnessed to generate hydroelectric power. It was built in conjunction with Siemens-Schuckert, the German company where McLaughlin had worked. The Minister for Industry and Commerce, Patrick McGilligan noted in 1928: 'We were not going to be debarred from bringing in foreign brains and skills at the beginning when we knew that we had not them at home'. Many of the engineers and workers were German. Construction on the plant began in 1925 and was completed in 1929, with the Electricity Supply Board (ESB) set up in 1927. By 1936/37 the plant was supplying 87 per cent of electricity demand in Ireland. The Shannon scheme was much more than a feat of engineering; it was tied up with notions of national self-sufficiency, the expansion of industry and Ireland's place among the modern nations.

The Ardnacrusha plant may have been the biggest but it was by no means the first hydroelectric plant in Ireland. Carlow, for instance, had a hydroelectric scheme which was opened by Charles Stuart Parnell on an electioneering visit in 1891. Bray had commenced its scheme that same year, Larne and Kilkenny the following year and Galway in 1897.

DUBLIN INSTITUTE OF ADVANCED STUDIES

The Dublin Institute of Advanced Studies, founded in 1940, was established through the efforts of Éamon de Valera, who was always keen for any opportunity to show that the fledgling state he was leading was a worthy member of the family of nations. An Institute of Advanced Studies had already been set up in Princeton University, as a safe haven for scientists like Albert Einstein fleeing the Nazi regime. De Valera, prudently aware that hosting research in mathematics and languages cost little, decided that a similar world-class institute should be set up in Dublin. The influence of de Valera was everywhere: a former mathematics teacher, who retained a lifelong interest in the subject, and a keen supporter of the Irish language, it was decided that the Institute would have a School of Theoretical Physics and a School of Celtic Studies.

Impressively, de Valera persuaded one of the founders of quantum theory to serve as director of the Institute. Erwin Schrödinger was teaching at a university in his native Austria. His main contribution to quantum physics was an equation which to this day is the starting point of almost any problem

in the field. He also contributed a famous thought experiment involving a cat which would involve more explanation than this little book allows! Although not Jewish himself, his outspoken criticism of Nazism led to him being fired in 1939 and fleeing to Rome. Suspicious that the national post would be checked, he sent letters from the Vatican seeking help. An answer came from de Valera, who was in Geneva in his capacity as president of the League of Nations assembly. The Irish consul in Rome arranged for Schrödinger and his wife Anny's passage from Rome to Geneva and on to Ireland. They arrived in October 1939.

Whilst his unconventional personal life (he lived with both Anny and another woman, Hilde, with whom he had a daughter, Ruth) had caused problems in Oxford and Princeton, de Valera apparently had no qualms about providing additional visas for Hilde and Ruth. Schrödinger spent seventeen years in Dublin (where his love life, it must be said, became even more complicated) until his retirement, whereupon he returned to Austria.

As for the Institute, it flourished as a centre for theoretical physics. A School of Cosmic Physics was added. Walter Heitler, one of the founders of quantum chemistry, was made professor in 1941 and both he and Schrödinger attracted many distinguished visitors. The institute did not cater for undergraduates, but many of the next generation of European physicists passed through as post-doctoral researchers. The Institute later became a renowned centre for the study of Einstein's relativity and later still the theory of elementary particles. De Valera was elected as an honorary member of the Royal Society of London in 1968 for his contribution to science in setting up the Institute.

IRELAND'S FIRST ...

Computer
Ireland's first computer was bought by the Comhlucht Siúicre Éireann, the Irish Sugar Company, in 1957 and installed in its factory outside Thurles. It was a Hollerith Electronic Computer 4 or HEC4 (later called the ICL1201) bought from the British Tabulating Machine Company. It was used to calculate payments owed to farmers for their crop load. It was moved to Dublin in 1969 along with the computer staff of twenty-seven people.

Railway
Ireland's first railway was the Dublin to Dun Laoghaire line opened in 1834. It was also the world's first suburban commuter railway. It was designed and built by the great engineer William Dargan (1799-1867).

Flight
Richard Crosbie was the first Irishman to fly. An inveterate inventor as a child, while he was at student at Trinity College, Dublin, in 1783 he heard of two Frenchmen who had spent twenty-five minutes elevated in the basket of a hot-air balloon. Richard felt he could go one better and cross the Irish sea. He held an exhibition in Ranelagh Gardens, south of Dublin city centre,

inviting people to pay to see his balloon. He cut the ropes and released it into the heavens, with a cat on board. The balloon made it to the coast of Scotland and was eventually recovered near the Isle of Man. For the next flight, Crosbie himself would be on board. The event was extremely popular with demand so high that tickets were forged. On 19 January 1785 Crosbie undertook his flight. Ever the showman he was dressed in a long, fur-lined robe of oiled silk, breeches of white quilted satin and a leopard skin cap, while his balloon was decorated with paintings of the Roman goddess of wisdom; Mercury, the messenger of the gods; and the Irish coat of arms. In front of a crowd of 20,000 Crosbie took off into the Dublin skies. He disappeared into a cloud after three and a half minutes. He only made it as far as Clontarf. A statute commemorates his daring endeavour in Ranelagh gardens.

10

WARS AND REBELLIONS

(NON) INVASIONS

Ireland, as most people are aware, has been subject to various invasions, conquests and settlements. The Celtic, Viking, Anglo-Norman and English invasions and settlements form crucial junctures in the country's history. But what of the invasions that Ireland escaped?

Romans

The Roman occupation of Britain stopped at the Scottish Highlands. Agricola, the leader of the Scottish campaign, established forts along the coast facing Ireland and from there looked across the water. His son-in-law Tacitus tells us that he 'saw that Ireland ... conveniently situated for the ports of Gaul might prove a valuable acquisition'. It also appears that a king, expelled from Ireland during a power struggle, was received by Agricola who hoped to make some use of him in a subsequent invasion. Tacitus recounts: 'I have often heard Agricola declare that a single legion, with a moderate band of auxiliaries, would be enough to finish the conquest of Ireland'. Perhaps the king was telling the powerful Roman general what he wanted to hear or jealously downplaying the strength of his countrymen? The Roman conquest of Hibernia was never attempted.

Nazis

During the Second World War there were fears that Ireland might be invaded by the Nazis prior to an assault on mainland Britain. Ireland had declared itself neutral, but this was a very real fear. And Ireland was vulnerable. The Director of Counter-Intelligence at MI5 was told in May 1940 that Irish resistance would not last one week if the Germans landed. This is not surprising given the available bodies and weapons: even after a recruitment drive there were only 13,500 men in the army by May 1940; the air corps had six slow-flying Lysanders and three old Gloster Gladiator fighter biplanes; the navy consisted of an armed trawler and *Muirchú* (this was in fact the renamed *Helga*, the infamous gunboat that had been used against the 1916 rebels but which the State had subsequently bought from the British). The Germans did draw up an invasion plan, Operation Green, in support of Operation Sea Lion (the plan to invade the UK). The British drew up Plan W, a planned occupation of the Free State by British forces, in secret with the Irish government, to counteract a German invasion.

INVASIONS

Normans

One invasion that very definitely took place was the Norman invasion in 1169. The cause was the rivalry between Tigernán Ua Ruairc (Tiernán O'Rourke), King of Bréifne, and Diarmait MacMurchada (Dermot MacMurrough), King of Leinster. In 1152, while he was away on a pilgrimage to the holy island of St Patrick on Lough Derg, Tiernán's young wife Derbforgaill was abducted from his castle by MacMurrough and his men. Tiernán went straight to the High King, Turlough O'Connor and demanded revenge. They raised an army and attacked MacMurrough's castle at Ferns and recovered Derbforgaill. That is one explanation for MacMurrough's deposition. There is another explanation stating that he lost his kingdom after his failed bid to become High King in 1166.

Either way, MacMurrough went to England where he asked Henry II to come to his aid in recovering his kingdom. Henry granted him permission to recruit soldiers in his dominion. The most significant ally he recruited was Richard fitz Gilbert, or 'Strongbow'. MacMurrough offered his daughter Aoife to Strongbow to secure the alliance.

So it was that the Normans came Ireland by invitation and, after them, Henry II, who decided he had better rein in Strongbow's apparent Irish ambitions.

REBELLIONS

Emmet's Rebellion, 1803

Emmet, in the process of trying to enlist French military help for a rebellion, met Napoleon (then First Counsel rather than Emperor) in Paris. They found themselves disagreeing hotly about the Act of Union of 1801 by which Ireland came to be governed directly by Westminster as part of the United Kingdom. Napoleon felt the fact that the Act had been passed without much public opposition proved that the Irish accepted the Act and their place in the Empire. Emmet disagreed but this did highlight a concern of his: that the mildness of the post-Union governance of Ireland might lead to a general acceptance of the Union.

The rebellion was an infamous logistical failure but not for want of planning: the rebels had begun manufacturing weapons and explosives in 1802, including a pike fitted with a hinge that would allow it to be folded and concealed under a cloak. The rebellion took place on 23 July, being brought forward after an explosion at an arms depot on Patrick Street on 16 July. Emmet had intended to rise in August, by which time he expected a French landing. Only a small minority of the expected insurgents from Dublin and its surrounds assembled. Many Kildare rebels turned back because of a provision that they would fight only if firearms were provided; the Wicklow rebels did not arrive at all. The attack on Dublin Castle was

abandoned after the group of insurgents led by Emmet came across the carriage of Lord Chief Justice Kilwarden on their way and dragged him out and killed him savagely. The alarm was raised at the castle by his daughter and the rebels dispersed. About 300 men took over Thomas Street and James's Street for about two hours.

One of most famous aspects of the rebellion was the bravery of Emmet's housekeeper while Emmet was in hiding. He had fled into the Wicklow Mountains as the rebellion unravelled. Anne Devlin, prodded with bayonets until she bled declared, 'I have nothing to tell. I will tell nothing'. They put a noose around her neck and she told them they could murder her without her breaking silence. They half-hanged her until she fainted but still she did not talk. Emmet was captured on 25 August.

Emmet delivered one of the most famous speeches in Irish history from the dock at his trial. Determining what he actually said is somewhat problematic: there are over seventy versions of the text in existence and some sections are almost certainly later additions. The famous last words come in varying forms but are at least generally accepted to have been uttered: 'When my country takes her place among the nations of the earth, then shall my character be vindicated, then may my epitaph be written'. Whether, as Eamon Dunphy suggested, the moment arrived for the engraver to sharpen his chisel when Ireland qualified for the quarter finals of the 1990 World Cup, is a matter for debate. However, even if that was the moment, the lack of a gravestone on which to carve the epitaph would have posed problems. The whereabouts of Emmet's body is unknown. He was publicly executed on 20 September. The remains were taken to Newgate Prison and then to Kilmainham Gaol where the jailer was told to bury the body in a nearby hospital's burial grounds if nobody claimed it. The body wasn't claimed, probably because of fears of arrest (members of Emmet's family and friends had been arrested, including those who had no involvement with the rebellion). However, a later search found no remains at this site. It is believed that it was removed although the location is a subject of speculation.

The 1916 Rising

The history of 1916 is well-trodden historical ground. But there are some lesser known facts (fifty of which have been compiled by Mick O'Farrell in *50 Things You Didn't Know About 1916* which remind us that the rebellion was of its own unique time.

The rebellion took place in various locations across the country but Dublin city was the main site of activity, and it was here, in key city centre locations like the GPO on O'Connell Street and St Stephen's Green, that the main action took place. The rebels took over these locations and what ensued was a series of stand-offs with the British Army over the course of seven days. The British bombed the rebels, the rebels shot back with whatever ammunition they had. People might assume that this fighting cleared the streets, particularly given the amount of crossfire that this type of combat entailed. In fact, looters took to the area around O'Connell Street early in the week, inspiring acts of giddy theft that perhaps can only be excused when law and

order break down. As detailed by O'Farrell, one observer noted
that a particularly enthusiastic (and stylish) thief 'went into
an abandoned tram-car ... stripped his rags off ... When he
reappeared, swaggering up and down the street, he was wearing
brown boots, a dress-suit, a Panama hat and carrying a lady's
sunshade'. Looting continued despite the rebels' best efforts to
curtail it, and only ceased once fires drove people away.

Quite aside from opportunists capitalising on the fight for Irish
freedom, there interested civilians gathered on the streets, eager
to get a close-up look at the fighting. As the newspapers were out
of circulation for Easter Week, this first-hand observation was
the only way to find out what was going on. Such was the level
of interest that the Volunteers in the GPO apparently struggled to
get provisions into the building through the crowds. There is even
an account of a ceasefire being caused by the panicked reaction of
civilians on Dame Street who found themselves a bit too close to
a British attack on a rebel outpost, the combatants yelling at the
fleeing and fainting people from the rooftops. Although precise
figures are not available, there were sadly a considerable number
of civilian deaths: possibly about 250, compared with 64 rebels.
There were many more – about 2,200 – wounded.

According to O'Farrell, one group who were shielded from the
harm of crossfire, despite being in the middle of the action, were
the ducks in Stephen's Green. At this site, the Irish Citizen Army
and some Volunteers pitted themselves against British forces.
Every day the park-keeper – James Kearney – left his house in
the green to feed the ducks and both sides would cease fire to
allow him. The ducks were, apparently, 'very little perturbed by
the bullets flying over their heads'.

On the rebel side, some of the soldiers were very young. Tommy
Keenan was twelve years old when he marched with the Irish
Citizen Army on Easter Monday. He was ordered home to report
to his parents, whereupon his father (quite understandably) locked
him in his room. Tommy escaped by climbing out of a window
and shimmying down a drainpipe to re-join the ICA in the Royal
College of Surgeons. On the British side the youngest casualty
was a sixteen year, Private Neville Nicholas Fryday of the 75th
Battalion Canadian Infantry. He was born in Thurles, County

Tipperary and his parents lived in Skankill, County Dublin, which according to O'Farrell notes means he may have been on leave visiting them when he became embroiled in the fighting.

PIRATES

The Sack of Baltimore

Baltimore County Cork was the site of the one of the more extraordinary attacks on Irish soil. In June 1631, a raid by a group of pirates from Algiers resulted in the kidnapping of over 100 people. Baltimore at this time was inhabited mainly by English settlers, drawn to the lucrative pilchard fishery which they had leased from the local O'Driscoll chieftain. A group of pirates, a mixture of Dutch, Turkish and Algerian, set sail from Algiers under a Dutchman called Murat Reis the Younger. They captured a number of smaller vessels, including one captained by a Dungarvan man called Jack Hackett. Hackett, in a bid to secure his own freedom, piloted the corsairs to the vulnerable settlement of Baltimore. Indeed, the target may have been Kinsale but Hackett apparently declared that town too risky. There, before dawn on 20 June, they raided the village, ultimately taking 107 men, women and children who were sold into the North African slave market. Three women were ransomed up to fourteen years after their abduction; the rest disappeared without trace. Many would have ended up as galley slaves or concubines in the harems of Algiers. While this might have been a straightforward opportunistic ransacking, an alternative theory is that Sir Walter Coppinger, who had wanted to take the village from the O'Driscolls and the settlers into his own control, may have manufactured the raid. His aims were ultimately realised, either way. Hackett, meanwhile, was arrested and hanged from a cliff top above the village. Many of the remaining villagers moved inland to Skibereen, so the raid had a role to play in the history of that nearby town. The incident is commemorated in a poem by Thomas Davis, *The Sack of Baltimore*.

OTHER PEOPLE'S FIGHTS

William Brown

The Irish took part in various wars of independence in Latin America. Indeed, an Irishman is considered one of the founding fathers of the Argentinian nation. William Brown was born in Foxford, County Mayo, in 1777. His family emigrated to Pennsylvania when he was nine and after his father's death a couple of years later, he found work as a cabin boy on a merchant ship. There followed a period as a sailor in the British Royal Navy and the Merchant Navy, and marriage, before he and his wife settled in Buenos Aires where he worked as a merchant-trader. Argentina began its war of independence against Spain in 1810, and in 1814 Brown became Commander-in-Chief of the navy, helping to secure his adopted country's freedom. He returned to the navy twice more, steering Argentina to victory over Brazil and Uruguay before retiring in 1845. On hearing about the Famine, Brown returned to Foxford in 1847. There is a museum in his honour there now, along with a statue in Dublin's Docklands presented by the Argentinian navy. The Argentinians have been very fulsome in their honouring of their naval leader: two towns, more than 1,200 streets, 500 statues, a city, five Argentine destroyers, an Antarctic naval base and at least four soccer clubs bear his name. He died in 1857 and is buried in La Recoleta Cemetery, Buenos Aries along with Eva Peron.

Batallón of San Patricio

The Batallón of San Patricio which fought during the Mexican-American War of 1846–48 is widely remembered in Mexico today for its bravery. John Riley, originally of Clifden but in the US Army at the time, defected and formed the unit before war was even declared. Within a year the 'Los San Patricios' were joined by Irish and German Catholics who deserted the US Army and Catholic foreigners resident in Mexico City who fought under a flag emblazoned with the Mexican coat of arms, an image of St Patrick and the words '*Erin go braugh* [*sic*]' (a flag said to have been designed by Riley). The 'San Patricios' distinguished themselves in a two particular battles and after the war were captured and court-martialled. Thirty were hanged.

Bolívar

Not all Irish contributions to Latin-American wars were showered in glory. An Irish Legion of mercenaries was raised in Dublin, London and elsewhere by an Irishman, John Devereux to fight with Simón Bolívar against Spanish rule. They sailed from Liverpool in 1819. There was no commissariat organisation on board the ships, meaning that provisions were not organised, and part of the force perished. Arriving on the island of Margarita off the Venezuelan coat, many died of disease and starvation. They took part in winning the city of Río Hacha in Columbia, raising their harp-emblazoned flag in place of the Spanish one. Eventually, the mercenaries frustrated by lack of pay and hunger, the episode descended into drinking, ransacking and looting. Most left for Jamaica while Bolívar was 'pleased to be rid of these mercenaries who would do no killing until they had first been paid for it'. Some other of the men remained loyal and proceeded with the campaign, among them some very competent soldiers, not least Lieutenant-Colonel Francis Burdett O'Connor, an excellent leader who led the remaining troops and ended up spending twenty years in Bolívar's army. There was also Daniel Florence O'Leary, who became Bolívar's aide-de-camp and served in Venezuela, Panama, Ecuador, Peru and Bolivia. His memoirs were published posthumously by his son, Simón Bolívar O'Leary.

Devereux himself arrived late and, while he made a handsome profit from his endeavour, escaped having to fight. This is perhaps unsurprising given that he was a charlatan and opportunist of the highest order who, despite what he had told Bolívar, had no military experience. His life story is unclear but it seems he was forced into exile in the United States after his father was involved in the 1798 rebellion, though he claimed to have been exiled for his own activities. There he ended up working as a merchant in Baltimore. In 1812 he turned up in Paris and, claiming to be from the United States government, secured the release of several confiscated cargoes held in the port of Naples. He returned to Baltimore with his fortune. Hearing of the wars of independence in South America he loaded up a schooner with arms and ammunition and set sail for Cartagena with the aim of selling his cargo. Bolívar was impressed and Devereux convinced him that he could raise a legion of 5,000. He returned to Ireland where, as part of his efforts, he drew the obvious parallels between the Irish freedom struggle and those of the South Americans. The Irish press spread the word of this great advocate of freedom and Daniel O'Connell supported the recruitment. In fact, his son Morgan joined the legion.

Devereux offered potential recruits four pence in the shilling more than the British Army, passage with 60 pesos on arrival; generous provisions including 1lb of beef or pork and 1 noggin of whisky a day; a proportionate share of land, capture and prize money; 200 acres of land with full discharge, leave to sell the land and passage home after five years. He sold the commissions for his legion and amassed a huge sum of £60,000 of which £7,000 was spent on ships and provisions. The drive, which lasted from 1819 to 1821, was successful. Over 1,700 enlisted and they received an energetic send off from Dublin with crowds following the ship down the Liffey and cheering. The selection process may not have been rigorous. On their arrival at Margarita, one observer described the soldiers as 'a confused, heterogeneous mass, varying from the peasant fresh from the plough-share, to the artisan, whose close, sedentary occupation rendered him sickly and altogether unfit for the active duty of a soldier'. As noted, this was not entirely fair and many served very successfully.

By 1820 stories of the treatment and behaviour of the soldiers had reached home which seemed to besmirch the notion of Irishmen as brave and honourable defenders of liberty. While some returning deserters blamed South American leaders, others blamed Irish officers. A public inquiry was set up in 1820 to investigate accusations against Devereux and his associates.

At this point Devereux went to South America. He was received with great pomp in Margarita and at a banquet in his honour he apparently delivered a stately two-hour address to the locals promising that all of Ireland was roused in support of their cause. He spoke in English, which none of the audience understood. He was given a position on Bolívar's staff where he remained until 1824, though he appears to have spent his time collecting money the government owed him. When he returned to Europe as Columbian envoy extraordinary to the courts of northern Europe, he had amassed a fortune of £150,000. His enemies were never able to bring him to book and he continued to earn vast wealth in the mercantile trade between Europe and South America. In 1840 he returned to New Granada and successfully petitioned for a state petition. He died in America in 1854.

So much for Devereux's Irish Legion. A different kind of Legion arrived over 100 years later. Séamus Grace and Alfie Lamb of the Legion of Mary arrived in 1953 and spread the organisation all around Columbia where it was popular amongst the poor. It thereafter moved into Ecuador, Venezuela and elsewhere in South America.

Eliza Lynch

Eliza Lynch was born in Charleville, County Cork in 1834 and, after a disastrous first marriage, ended up in Paris where she became the lover of Francisco Solano Lopez, heir to the dictatorship of Paraguay. She returned to Paraguay with him and became a dictator's mistress. Lopez embarked on the war of the Triple Alliance against Brazil, Argentina and Uruguay (1864–70) during which an astonishingly awful 90 per cent of Paraguayan men and 50 per cent of the women died. When Brazilian forces entered Asuncion in January 1869, Eliza, Lopez and their children fled. The final standoff came in March 1870 when both Lopez and the eldest son were killed. In a ragged ball gown and dancing slippers, Eliza buried them with her bare hands.

Claiming British citizenship, Eliza was deported to Europe. The Paraguayan government declared her an outlaw and stripped her of all her possessions: she was the biggest landowner in the country, having acquired about a third of the national territory in her own name. She returned in 1875. She was welcomed by the masses, with whom she had always been popular, but a group of aristocratic women wanted her arraigned or expelled. She returned to Paris where she died in 1886.

That opposing reaction to her return in 1875 encapsulates the polarising opinions of her. By one interpretation she is the evil genius inciting Lopez's Napoleonic ambitions and horrific war and by another interpretation powerless to oppose an increasingly paranoid man, teetering on the edge of insanity. In 1961, the dictator General Alfredo Stroessner had her remains brought back to Asuncion, declaring her Paraguay's national heroine. The tragic war of the Triple Alliance is itself seen both as an act of unjustifiable self-indulgence by Lopez and, by complete contrast, as a heroic act of national defence. If ever a person became caught up in the maelstrom of history and historical interpretation, it is Eliza Lynch.

Cuba

Ireland can claim an indirect role in the Cuban Revolution via the Argentinian Che Guevara's grandmother, Anna Lynch. Anna was the daughter of Patrick Lynch, born in County Galway. Her son Ernesto (Che's father) said in 1969: 'The first thing to note is that in my son's veins flowed the blood of Irish rebels. Che inherited some of the features of our restless ancestors. There was something in his nature which drew him to distant wandering, dangerous adventures and new ideas'.

As a footnote, that famous image of Che Guevara that has graced posters and t-shirts the world over was the work of an Irishman, Jim Fitzpatrick. Fitzpatrick had served Guevara a drink in a bar in Kilkee in 1961: Che and his band of revolutionaries were on a (fog-delayed) stop-over at Shannon en route from Prague to Havana. Based on a photograph by Alberto Korda, Fitzpatrick created the image in 1960 and doctored it to give him longer hair and more upward turning eyes; the former because it was more in tune with the 1960s rebellion, the latter perhaps because it made him look more saintly. Fitzpatrick has never claimed royalties for the use of the image.

The Risorgimento

Italy, until the mid-nineteenth century, was a series of statelets. The unification movement of the 1850s led by Garibaldi and Mazzini amongst others, known as the Risorgimento, had the annexing of the Papal States as a key aim. Pope Pius IX, vulnerable without a viable army, called on the Catholics of Europe to raise an army defence. By January 1860 Papal emissaries had arrived in Ireland and the call to arms went out from pulpits up and down the land. The British government, looking to undermine the influence of Austria and France in Italian affairs, were in favour of unification. In response to the Church's call to arms, the government passed the Foreign Enlistment Act, barring British subjects from joining foreign armies. This only encouraged nationalists further.

In total, about 1,400 Irishmen, amongst them labourers, farmers, doctors and lawyers, travelled to Italy. Many were forced to travel in groups disguised as pilgrims and accompanied by priests. Most had arrived by late June 1860 to find themselves undergoing hasty training with nine other nationalities where English was not amongst the three designated languages of the Papal army. The promised uniforms from Ireland never arrived and they were issued with surplus Austrian uniforms and obsolete weapons. The Battalion of St Patrick was formed. It was split into companies however and did not fight as a unit.

By all accounts the Irish fought fiercely and bravely over the eighteen days in September that constituted the Papal War of 1860. They lost the war but returned to Ireland as heroes. A small number (the Irish contingent never numbered more than fifty) remained to take up positions in the newly formed Company of St Patrick, part of a smaller, reorganised Papal army. Many of these left to fight for Abraham Lincoln in a American Civil War which broke out the following year and the Company was disbanded shortly afterwards.

Violet Gibson

Although not quite an intervention in another country's war, Violet Gibson did come close to ending Italian fascism on 7 April 1926 when she shot Benito Mussolini as he left an engagement with the International Congress of Surgeons. She shot at point-blank range but he turned his head. He set off for Libya soon after with a sticking plaster on his nose. In 1926, Mussolini was being feted by the British press for his work in suppressing communism and had just been awarded the Order of Bath by the King. Violet, then fifty years old, was born in Dublin, the daughter of Lord Ashbourne, the Lord Chancellor of Ireland. Born into a Protestant family, she had come to embrace, variously, Irish nationalism, Christian Science, theosophy and, eventually, Catholicism. It was a version of Catholicism, however, that did not rule out killing. She attempted to shoot herself once and repeatedly threatened to attack the pope whom she saw as a totalitarian dictator.

On the day of the assassination attempt, the police saved Violet from being killed by an angry mob of Mussolini supporters with the dictator himself, careful not to be seen executing or imprisoning a fifty-year-old woman, let her go. She never gave a reason for the assassination attempt. She spent the remainder of her life in a lunatic asylum in England.

WOMEN WARRIORS

Queen Maeve and the Brown Bull of Cooley

There are probably few other countries where wars are begun over cattle. Queen Maeve was the warrior Queen of Connacht. According to the legend, she was proud of the fact that she equalled her husband Ailill in wealth and power. The only trump card he held was a magnificent bull. There was only one bull in Ireland that could rival Ailill's bull, and Meave was determined to get it. The Brown Bull of Cooley, however, belonged to the King of Ulster. Not deterred, Maeve raised an army and marched to Cooley. Confronted by Cuchulainn, the hero of the Red Knights of Ulster, a battle ensued in which Maeve's army was defeated. She did manage to steal the bull, however, and take it back to Connacht. When the Brown Bull and Ailill's bull were introduced, they fought each other to their mutual deaths. Maeve felt her honour was satisfied, if not quite in the manner she had intended. The cairn on top of Knocknarea, the hill that looms over Sligo town, is said to be Maeve's burial place. Removing a stone will bring terrible luck.

Grace O'Malley

Grace O'Malley is a historical figure around whom elements of the legendary swirl. If she had not existed, this warrior-queen might well have been invented by storytellers. She was born in the 1530s in County Mayo. According to one story her father refused to allow her to go on a trading mission to Spain as her long hair would get caught in the sails (in other words, the sea is not place for a woman). Her response was to shave her head, earning her the name Gráinne Mhaol ('*maol*' meaning bald).

She went on to command a fleet and was a fearsome pirate, trader and chieftain (she is often referred to as a 'pirate-queen'). She controlled the shipping along most the west coast, and made her fortune in the process.

Grace loved castles and acquired a number of them. One, Rockfleet Castle on the northern shore of Clew Bay in Mayo, was taken from her second husband Richard Burke. On marrying, they had agreed that either party could terminate the union after the first year. When the time came, Grace barricaded herself into Richard's castle and sent him packing. Their only son, Tibbot-na-Long, was said to have been born on one of his mother's galleys. When it was attacked the following day by Algerian corsairs, Grace rose from her bed and turned the battle around. So the legends go.

Determined to retain control of her property and wealth, she was not shy of a fight. In one defence of a castle she had the lead from the roof torn off, melted and poured on the attackers' heads. When the Lord President of Connacht attacked Rockfleet in 1574, she and her husband were triumphant after a three-week siege. It was also said she had a long chain from her favourite ship tied to her bedpost, lest anyone try to steal it.

By 1593, the Governor of Connacht, Richard Bingham, had confiscated Grace's lands and imprisoned her son Tibbot. She travelled to petition Queen Elizabeth I; the only Gaelic woman ever to be received at court. The meeting was conducted in Latin as Grace spoke little English and the Queen no Irish. Grace was apparently offered a handkerchief and after using it, threw it in the fire. When the queen told her that it was meant to be put in her pocket, Grace declared that where she came they had higher standards of hygiene than to keep a soiled handkerchief on their person.

Elizabeth agreed to the release of Tibbot and ordered that provision be made for Grace for the rest of her life out of her sons' estates. In return, she expected Grace to behave as a dutiful subject. 'She showeth herself dutiful, although she hath in former times lived out of order' wrote Elizabeth after the meeting. Perhaps unsurprisingly, however, this independent woman soon joined with the Gaelic lords' rebellion known as the Nine Years War. She died in 1603 and is buried on Clare Island.

An extra place is always laid at the dinner table in Howth Castle for Grace O'Malley. According to the story, Grace stopped off at Howth harbour on her way back from visiting Queen Elizabeth in London (the date is given as 1575 but she did not visit the queen until 1593 though she did visit the Lord Deputy in Dublin in 1576). She arrived at the castle but was refused entry. Outraged at this breach of ancient customs of hospitality, the hot-headed O'Malley abducted the castle's heir and took the boy to her own stronghold of Rockfleet on Clew Bay. Her ransom demand was that Howth Castle would keep its doors open at meal times and a place be set for an unexpected guest. The Lord of Howth agreed and the pledge is still kept to this day.

Countess Constance Georgine Markievecz

Countess Constance Georgine Markievecz set some records on behalf of Irish women. She was the first woman to be elected to Westminster in the 1919 election, though as a Sinn Féin TD she refused to take her seat. Instead she became the first female cabinet post holder in the world, serving as Minister for Labour in the First Dáil formed after that same election of 1919. She trained as a painter. However, politics became her life: a suffragist, socialist and Sinn Féiner, she fought in 1916 and was imprisoned for her efforts. During the Rising she barricaded herself in to the Royal College of Surgeons with 120 men and kissed her revolver before handing it over to her captors on their surrender.

CONCLUSION

Countless thousands of facts have been omitted from this book for which it is possible to plead only this: there are countless thousands of facts. It was hoped to give a flavour of the diversity, oddness, commonness, backwardness and forwardness of Ireland. Of course, to view any country as a collection of facts would be to do it a vast disservice. There is a beating heart somewhere in all things, countries included, that has to be felt rather than read.

> Did sea define the land or land the sea?
> Each drew new meaning from the waves' collision.
> Sea broke on land to full identity.

Seamus Heaney, 'Lovers on Aran'